LIVING BUDDHA,

LIVING CHRIST

OTHER BOOKS
BY THICH NHAT HANH

A

Riverhead Book

1995

LIVING BUDDHA,

LIVING CHRIST

Thich Nhat Hanh

INTRODUCTION BY ELAINE PAGELS

FOREWORD BY
BROTHER DAVID STEINDL-RAST, O.S.B.

RIVERHEAD BOOKS
a division of G. P. Putnam's Sons
Publishers Since 1838
a member of
Penguin Putnam Inc.
375 Hudson Street
New York, NY 10014

Library of Congress Cataloging-in-Publication Data

Nh'ât Hạnh, Thích.
Living Buddha, living Christ / Thich Nhat Hanh.
p.   cm.
ISBN 1-57322-018-3 (alk. paper)
BR128.B8N43   1995
294.3'37—dc20   95-24014   CIP

Book design by Gretchen Achilles

Printed in the United States of America

40 39 38 37

This book is printed on acid-free paper. ∞

ACKNOWLEDGMENTS

I am grateful to my friends Martin Pitt, Mobi Warren, and Arnold Kotler for their valuable time and energy in helping to transcribe tapes and edit this book, making it into a wonderful instrument for dialogue.

CONTENTS

FOREWORD

Twice in this book Thich Nhat Hanh puts before us a powerful image of Christian legend: In midwinter, St. Francis is calling out to an almond tree, "Speak to me of God!" and the almond tree breaks into bloom. *It comes alive.* There is no other way of witnessing to God but by aliveness. With a fine instinct, Thich Nhat Hanh traces genuine aliveness to its source. He recognizes that this is what the biblical tradition calls the Holy Spirit. After all, the very word "spirit" means "breath," and to breathe means to live. The Holy Spirit is the breath of divine life.

This conjures up the Bible story of creation: In the beginning, the Spirit of God—always feminine in the Bible—hovers like a mother bird over the lifeless chaos, brooding and bringing forth life in all its forms and degrees. "For the Spirit of the Lord fills the whole universe and holds all things together . . ." (Wisdom 1:7) At the end of this creation myth, we see God, in a touching image, breathe life into the nostrils of the still-lifeless human figure formed out of earth in God's own image. And so we humans come alive. From the biblical perspective, there has never been a human being who is not alive with God's own life breath.

We Christians have no monopoly on the Holy Spirit: "All those who are led by the Spirit of God are [daughters and] sons of God." (Romans 8:14) No wonder, then, that a Buddhist who is not afraid of the pain it brings to be truly alive—birth pain, growing pain—should recognize the Holy Spirit as the ultimate source of all aliveness. "The Spirit blows where she wills." (John 3:8) And no wonder that alive Christians recognize their sisters and brothers in the Holy Spirit anywhere.

"Nhat Hanh is my brother," wrote Thomas Merton. "We are both monks, and we have lived the monastic life about the same number of years. We are both poets, both existentialists. I have far more in common with Nhat Hanh than I have with many Americans." That was written when the two peacemakers confronted together the catastrophe of the Vietnam War. It was at that time that I myself had the privilege of meeting Thich Nhat Hanh, known to friends and students as Thây (teacher), and I recognized in him a brother in the Spirit.

Great was my joy to find on the very first page of this book a reference to Thây's sharing the Eucharist with Dan Berrigan. On one occasion, this took place in the small student's room I occupied at Columbia University. As one of the sacred readings that evening, Thây recited the Heart Sutra, the most important Zen scripture, in Vietnamese. It was on April 4, 1968. How could I forget that date! Afterwards we went to listen to a lecture by Hans Küng, but the event was interrupted by the shattering news that Dr. Martin Luther King, Jr., had been assassinated.

The ritual we had celebrated earlier that evening had once again been reenacted in history: "Greater love no one has but to lay down one's life for one's friends." (John 15:13) Jesus had done this 2,000 years ago; Martin had done it today; and Thây, in risking his own life to speak out uncompromisingly for peace in Vietnam, was allowing himself to walk in the same direction. "Nhat Hanh is a free man who has acted as a free man in favor of his brothers, moved by the spiritual dynamic of a tradition of religious compassion," Thomas Merton wrote. "We cannot let him go back to Saigon to be destroyed while we sit here cherishing the warm humanitarian glow of good intentions and worthy sentiments." In the end, Thây was spared. Although unable to return to Vietnam, he has lived in exile ever since. The roots of *Living Buddha, Living Christ* go back to that time when, in the face of death, human hearts were most alive.

"It is safer to approach God through the Holy Spirit than through theology," Thây writes. And yet he is a theologian in the deepest sense: He speaks of God out of his own living experience. And he speaks with enthusiasm—with the voice of the divine Spirit in his own heart. If we listen attentively, we will hear traditional truths expressed in startling new ways. And we might be surprised by Thây's sure sense for essentials. For Christian readers, it would be a great loss to overlook this voice of insight and compassion, insisting instead on academic niceties and theological precision.

"Discussing God is not the best use of our energy," Thich Nhat Hanh writes. "If we touch the Holy Spirit, we touch God not as a concept but as a living reality." With a gentle but firm hand, this monk leads us again and again from theory to practice. He has deep respect for concepts, but as a means, not an end. The Zen tradition has developed a rich and nuanced terminology, but its emphasis on practice makes it less likely that one will get stuck in notions. Thây insists: "Reality is free from all notions. . . . It is our duty to transcend words and concepts to be able to encounter reality."

He continues: "When we see someone overflowing with love and understanding, someone who is keenly aware of what is going on, we know that they are very close to the Buddha and to Jesus Christ." How would you feel if you met a person like that? Overjoyed? Of course. Comfortable. Perhaps not. I have had the privilege of encountering men and women close to the living Buddha, the living Christ—some of them world-famous, others completely unknown; it makes no difference. Their very presence awakens us and challenges our complacency.

Reading *Living Buddha, Living Christ,* I felt the same challenge. I am not referring to the few passages that criticize Christian (or rather un-Christian) narrowness, exclusivism, or sexism. Any Christian who strives to follow Christ will have voiced those criticisms long ago and possibly less gently. The challenge I felt was personal. It came not from anything Thây said, but from his silence, from between the lines. I felt a bit like the almond tree confronted by St. Francis. "Start blooming, frozen Christian!" the mystic Angelus Silesius called out. "Springtime is at hand. When will you ever bloom if not here and now?" Thich Nhat Hanh's words entered me like a Zen koan: Speak to me of the unspeakable, and not with words. "Speak to me of God!" This is the challenge Thich Nhat Hanh offers us: Come alive, truly alive!

—Brother David Steindl-Rast, O.S.B.
Big Sur, California
Trinity Sunday 1995

INTRODUCTION

In *Living Buddha, Living Christ,* Thich Nhat Hanh expresses deep respect and appreciation for many elements of Christian tradition—not only for the teachings of Jesus but even for the concept of the Trinity and the possibilities for experiencing the love and compassion that many Christians and certain Christian communities offer. Fortunately for his readers, however, Thich Nhat Hanh does not take the easy way out of ecumenical discussion by ignoring disagreement. He also points out elements of Christian tradition that foster religious intolerance and have led to religious hatred. Thich Nhat Hanh speaks of this from his own experience. From the time the French who colonized Vietnam allied themselves with Christian missionary efforts to the crisis of 1963 when President Diêm passed a law prohibiting his people from celebrating the Buddhist national holiday, many Vietnamese have understandably associated Christianity with foreign attempts to establish political and cultural domination.

With his characteristic directness, Thich Nhat Hanh goes to the heart of the matter. After examining the parallels between the theology of the Trinity and the Buddhist concept of "interbeing," he takes issue with the man regarded by millions as the foremost exponent of the Christian tradition—Pope John Paul II. In his recent book, *Crossing the Threshold of Hope,* John Paul II states that:

> Christ is absolutely original and absolutely unique. If He were only a wise man like Socrates, if He were a "prophet" like Mohammed, if He were "enlightened" like Buddha, without any doubt He would not be what He is. He is the one mediator between God and humanity.

Quoting this passage, Thich Nhat Hanh comments:

This statement does not seem to reflect the deep mystery of the oneness of the Trinity. It also does not reflect the fact that Christ is also the Son of Man. All Christians, while praying to God, address Him as Father. Of course Christ is unique. But who is not unique? Socrates, Mohammed, the Buddha, you, and I are all unique. The idea behind the statement, however, is the notion that Christianity provides the only way of salvation and all other religious traditions are of no use. This attitude excludes dialogue and fosters religious intolerance and discrimination. It does not help.

As one engaged in studying Christian tradition who also participates in Christian practice, I find myself agreeing with Thich Nhat Hanh at this and nearly every significant turn of *Living Buddha, Living Christ.* Yet my agreement does not come from immersion in Buddhist tradition—on the contrary, it comes from exploration into the earliest history of Christianity. As a graduate student, I was surprised to learn of a discovery that is still transforming our understanding of Christianity—and its mysterious founder. In 1947, when a Bedouin villager named Mohammed Ali was digging for bird-lime fertilizer under a cliff near the town of

Nag Hammadi in Upper Egypt, he struck something underground. Moments later he unearthed a
sealed earthenware jar, six feet high, and inside
were thirteen ancient codices, bound in tooled ga-
zelle leather. The collection included an astonish-
ing number of ancient Christian gospels and other
writings, including dialogues, conversation, and vi-
sions attributed to Jesus and His disciples. One of
these was the Gospel of Thomas, which Helmut
Koester, Professor of New Testament at Harvard
University, dates to c.50 C.E.—some twenty years
before any of the New Testament gospels were
written. Others were the Gospel of Philip, the
Dialogue of the Savior, the Secret Book of John,
and the Apocalypse of Paul—some fifty-two texts
in all. The books apparently were salvaged from
the library of the earliest Christian monastery in
Egypt after the archbishop of Alexandria ordered
the monks to destroy all books he deemed "heretical"—that is, Christian sources not endorsed by
the clerical authorities.

Voyaging from these gnostic Christian texts to
the work of Thich Nhat Hanh, I feel I am in familiar territory. During the formative era of the Christian movement (50-150 C.E.), many Christians spoke
from a perspective similar to his, seeing Jesus as one
through whom the divine was manifested, and

through whose example and teaching they could hope for similar enlightenment. But the majority of Christian church leaders rejected such teaching not only for the "blasphemy" of inviting each disciple to identify with Christ Himself but also for teaching what could prove confusing or destabilizing to many church members.

By investigating these long-hidden sources, we discover that the early Christian movement contained enormously more diversity of viewpoint and practice than most Christians later acknowledged or even imagined. One need only listen to the words of the Gospel of Thomas to hear how it resonates with the Buddhist tradition:

Jesus said, "If those who lead you say to you, 'Look, the Kingdom is in the sky,' then the birds of the sky will get there first. If they say, 'It is in the sea,' then the fish will get there first. Rather, the Kingdom is inside of you, and it is outside of you. When you come to know yourselves, then you will become known, and you will realize that *it is you who are the children of the living Father.* But if you will not know yourselves, then you dwell in poverty, and it is you who are that poverty" (emphasis added).

According to the Gospel of Thomas, that "living Jesus" indeed offers access to God, but instead of claiming to be the "*only begotten* Son of God" (as the New Testament Gospel of John will later insist), He reveals that "it is you who are the children of God." This gospel is attributed to "Thomas the twin." The name Thomas in Hebrew literature means "twin." Did Jesus, then, have a twin brother? I suggest instead that the attribution, meant symbolically, directs the reader to discover that he—or she—is, indeed, at a deep level, Jesus' "twin"—and fellow child of God. As the gospel closes, Jesus goes on to speak directly to Thomas:

> Whosoever drinks from my mouth *will become as I am; and I will become that person;* and the mysteries will be revealed to him (emphasis added).

According to The Book of Thomas the Contender, another text from the same discovery, Jesus speaks to Thomas—that is, to the reader—in these words:

> Since it has been said that you are my twin and my true companion, it is not fitting for you to be ignorant of yourself. So while you accompany me, although you do not yet understand

it, you have already come to know, and you will be called "the one who knows himself." For whoever has not known himself knows nothing, but he who has known himself has already understood the depth of all things.

While the New Testament gospels speak of Jesus as the only door to salvation, the only path ("I am the way . . . no one come to the Father except through me" [John 14:6]), another of these texts, The Teaching of Silvanus, speaks quite differently:

Knock upon yourself as upon a door, and walk upon yourself as on a straight road. For if you walk on that path, you cannot go astray; and when you knock on that door, what you open for yourself shall open.

These ancient gospels tend to point beyond faith toward a path of solitary searching to find understanding, or *gnosis*. The Gospel of Thomas acknowledges that such exploration is simultaneously frustrating, troubling, and surprising:

Let the one who seeks not stop seeking until he finds. When he finds, he shall be troubled.

When he becomes troubled, he will be amazed, and shall come to transcend all things.

This gospel warns, too, that what is at stake is one's deepest well-being, or else one's destruction:

Jesus said, "If you bring forth what is within you, what you bring forth will save you. If you do not bring forth what is within you, what you do not bring forth will destroy you."

Although church leaders also charged gnostic Christians with spiritual elitism and with solipsism, the sources discovered at the Nag Hammadi, like Buddhist sources, direct the disciple toward loving compassion for others: According to the Gospel of Thomas, Jesus says, "Love your brother as the apple of your eye." The gnostic Gospel of Truth exhorts the hearer to

Speak of the truth with those who search for it, and of knowledge to those who have committed a sin in their error. Make firm the foot of those who have stumbled; give rest to those who are weary, and raise up those who wish to rise, and awaken those who sleep.

As I read *Living Buddha, Living Christ,* I wondered: Does Thich Nhat Hanh know the Gospel of Thomas and other gnostic sources or did he choose the term "living Christ"—a term more characteristic of gnostic texts than of the New Testament—by a kind of spiritual intuition? In either case, those who are more familiar than I am with Buddhist tradition, and especially those more experienced in meditation and contemplation, will surely notice in these ancient Christian sources many more resonances than I can mention here. Comparative study of Buddhism and early (gnostic) Christianity has barely begun. The publication of *Living Buddha, Living Christ* presents an opportune moment to deepen our understanding.

—Elaine Pagels
Princeton, New Jersey
June 23, 1995

LIVING BUDDHA,

LIVING CHRIST

ONE

BE STILL AND KNOW

RELIGIOUS LIFE IS LIFE

Twenty years ago at a conference I attended of theologians and professors of religion, an Indian Christian friend told the assembly, "We are going to hear about the beauties of several traditions, but that does not mean that we are going to make a fruit salad." When it came my turn to speak, I said, "Fruit salad can be delicious! I have shared the Eucharist with Father Daniel Berrigan, and our worship became possible because of the sufferings we Vietnamese and Americans shared over many years." Some of the

Buddhists present were shocked to hear I had participated in the Eucharist, and many Christians seemed truly horrified. To me, religious life is life. I do not see any reason to spend one's whole life tasting just one kind of fruit. We human beings can be nourished by the best values of many traditions.

Professor Hans Küng has said, "Until there is peace between religions, there can be no peace in the world." People kill and are killed because they cling too tightly to their own beliefs and ideologies. When we believe that ours is the only faith that contains the truth, violence and suffering will surely be the result. The second precept of the Order of Interbeing, founded within the Zen Buddhist tradition during the war in Vietnam, is about letting go of views: "Do not think the knowledge you presently possess is changeless, absolute truth. Avoid being narrow-minded and bound to present views. Learn and practice nonattachment from views in order to be open to receive others' viewpoints." To me, this is the most essential practice of peace.

❧

DIALOGUE: THE KEY TO PEACE

I have been engaged in peace work for more than thirty years: combating poverty, ignorance, and disease; going to sea to help rescue boat people; evacuating the wounded from combat zones; resettling refugees; helping hungry children and orphans; opposing wars; producing and disseminating peace literature; training peace and social workers; and rebuilding villages destroyed by bombs. It is because of the practice of meditation—stopping, calming, and looking deeply—that I have been able to nourish and protect the sources of my spiritual energy and continue this work.

During the war in Vietnam, I saw communists and anti-communists killing and destroying each other because each side believed they had a monopoly on the truth. Many Christians and Buddhists in our country were fighting each other instead of working together to stop the war. I wrote a booklet entitled "Dialogue: The Key to Peace," but my voice was drowned out by the bombs, mortars, and shouting. An American soldier standing on the back of a military truck spit on the head of my disciple, a young monk named Nhât Trí. The soldier must have thought we Buddhists were undermining America's war effort or that my disciple was a communist in disguise. Brother Nhât Trí became so angry that he thought about leaving the monastery and joining the National Liberation Front. Because I had been practicing meditation, I was able to see that everyone in the war was a victim, that the American soldiers who had been sent to Vietnam to bomb, kill, and destroy were also being killed and maimed. I urged Brother Nhât Trí to remember that the G.I. was also a war victim, the victim of a wrong view and a wrong policy, and I urged him to continue his work for peace as a monk. He was able to see that, and he became one of the most active workers in the Buddhist School of Youth for Social Service.

In 1966, I came to North America to try to help dissolve some of the wrong views that were at the root of the war. I met with hundreds of individuals and small groups, and also with members of Congress and Secretary of Defense Robert McNamara. The visit was organized by the Fellowship of Reconciliation, an interfaith peace organization, and many active Christians helped me in these efforts, among them Dr. Martin Luther King, Jr., Father Thomas Merton, and Father Daniel Berrigan. These were, in fact, the Americans I found it easiest to communicate with.

∞

TOUCHING JESUS

But my path to discovering Jesus as one of my spiritual ancestors was not easy. The colonization of my country by the French was deeply connected with the efforts of the Christian missionaries. In the late seventeenth century, Alexandre de Rhôdes, one of the most active of the missionaries, wrote in his *Cathechismus in Octo Dies Divisus:* "Just as when a cursed, barren tree is cut down, the branches that are still on it will also fall, when the sinister and deceitful Sakya [Buddha] is defeated, the idolatrous fabrications that proceed from him will also be destroyed." Later, in the late 1950s and early 1960s, Catholic Archbishop Ngo Dinh Thuc, in his efforts to evangelize Vietnam, leaned heavily on the political power of his brother, President Ngo Dinh Diêm. President Diêm's 1963 decree prohibiting the celebration of Wesak, the most important Buddhist national holiday, was the straw that broke our back. Tens of thousands of lay and ordained Buddhists demonstrated for religious freedom, leading to a coup d'état and the overthrow of the Diêm regime. In such an atmosphere of discrimination and injustice against non-Christians, it was difficult for me to discover the beauty of Jesus' teachings.

It was only later, through friendships with Christian men and women who truly embody the spirit of understanding and compassion of Jesus, that I have been able to touch the depths of Christianity. The moment I met Martin Luther King, Jr., I knew

I was in the presence of a holy person. Not just his good work but his very being was a source of great inspiration for me. And others, less well known, have made me feel that Lord Jesus is still here with us. Hebe Kohlbrugge, a beautiful Dutch woman who saved the lives of thousands of Jews during World War II, was so committed to helping Vietnamese orphans and other desperately needy children during the war that when her government refused to support this work, she gave them back her World War II medals. Reverend Heinz Kloppenburg, General Secretary of the German Fellowship of Reconciliation, also supported our humanitarian work. He was so kind and so open, I only needed to say a few words to him and he understood everything right away. Through men and women like these, I feel I have been able to touch Jesus Christ and His tradition.

∽

REAL COMMUNICATION

On the altar in my hermitage in France are images of Buddha and Jesus, and every time I light incense, I touch both of them as my spiritual ancestors. I can do this because of contact with these real Christians. When you touch someone who authentically represents a tradition, you not only touch his or her tradition, you also touch your own. This quality is essential for dialogue. When participants are willing to learn from each other, dialogue takes place just by their being together. When those who represent a spiritual tradition embody the essence of their tradition, just the way they walk, sit, and smile speaks volumes about the tradition.

In fact, sometimes it is more difficult to have a dialogue with people in our own tradition than with those of another tradition. Most of us have suffered from feeling misunderstood or even betrayed by those of our own tradition. But if brothers and sisters in the same tradition cannot understand and communicate with each other, how can they communicate with those outside their tradition? For dialogue to be fruitful, we need to live deeply our own tradition and, at the same time, listen deeply to others. Through the practice of deep looking and deep listening, we become free, able to see the beauty and values in our own *and* others' tradition.

Many years ago, I recognized that by understanding your own tradition better, you also develop increased respect, consideration, and understanding for others. I had had a naive thought, a kind of prejudice inherited from my ancestors. I thought that because Buddha had taught for forty-five years and Jesus for only two or three, that Buddha must have been a more accomplished teacher. I had that thought because I did not know the teachings of the Buddha well enough.

One day when he was thirty-eight years old, the Buddha met King Prasenajit of Kosala. The king said, "Reverend, you are young, yet people call you 'The Highest Enlightened One.' There are holy men in our country eighty and ninety years old, venerated by many people, yet none of them claims to be the highest enlightened one. How can a young man like you make such a claim?"

The Buddha replied, "Your majesty, enlightenment is not a matter of age. A tiny spark of fire has the power to burn down a whole city. A small poisonous snake can kill you in an instant. A baby prince has the potentiality of a king. And a young monk has the capacity of becoming enlightened and changing the world." We can learn about others by studying ourselves.

For any dialogue between traditions to be deep, we have to be aware of both the positive and negative aspects of our own tradition. In Buddhism, for example, there have been many schisms. One hundred years after the passing of the Buddha, the community of his disciples divided into two parts; within four hundred years, there were twenty schools; and since then, there have been many more. Fortunately, these separations have, for the most part, not been too painful, and the garden of Buddhism is now filled with many beautiful flowers, each school representing an attempt to keep the Buddha's teachings alive under new circumstances. Living organisms need to change and grow. By respecting the differences within our own church and seeing how these differences enrich one another, we are more open to appreciating the richness and diversity of other traditions.

In a true dialogue, both sides are willing to change. We have to appreciate that truth can be received from outside of—not only within—our own group. If we do not believe that, entering into dialogue would be a waste of time. If we think we monopolize the truth and we still organize a dialogue, it is not authentic. We have to believe that by engaging in dialogue with the other person, we have the possibility of making a change within ourselves, that we can become deeper. Dialogue is not a means for assimilation in the sense that one side expands and incorporates the other into its "self." Dialogue must be practiced on the basis of "non-self." We have to allow what is good, beautiful, and meaningful in the other's tradition to transform us.

But the most basic principle of interfaith dialogue is that the dialogue must begin, first of all, within oneself. Our capacity to make peace with another person and with the world depends very much on our capacity to make peace with ourselves. If we are at war with our parents, our family, our society, or our church, there is probably a war going on inside us also, so the most basic work for peace is to return to ourselves and create harmony among the elements within us—our feelings, our perceptions, and our mental states. That is why the practice of meditation, looking deeply, is so important. We must recognize and accept the conflicting elements that are within us and their underlying causes. It takes time, but the effort always bears fruit. When we have peace within, real dialogue with others is possible.

∞

INTERBEING

In the Psalms, it says, "Be still and know that I am God." "Be still" means to become peaceful and concentrated. The Buddhist term is *samatha* (stopping, calming, concentrating). "Know" means to acquire wisdom, insight, or understanding. The Buddhist term is *vipasyana* (insight, or looking deeply). "Looking deeply" means observing something or someone with so much concentration that the distinction between observer and observed disappears. The result is insight into the true nature of the object. When we look into the heart of a flower, we see clouds, sunshine, minerals, time, the earth, and everything else in the cosmos in it. Without clouds, there could be no rain, and there would be no flower. Without time, the flower could not bloom. In fact, the flower is made entirely of non-flower elements; it has no independent, individual existence. It "inter-is" with everything else in the universe. Interbeing is a new term, but I believe it will be in the dictionary soon because it is such an important word. When we see the nature of inter-being, barriers between ourselves and others are dissolved, and peace, love, and understanding are possible. Whenever there is understanding, compassion is born.

Just as a flower is made only of non-flower elements, Buddhism is made only of non-Buddhist elements, including Christian ones, and Christianity is made of non-Christian elements, including Buddhist ones. We have different roots, traditions, and ways of seeing, but we share the common qualities of love, understanding, and acceptance. For our dialogue to be open, we need to open our hearts, set aside our prejudices, listen deeply, and represent truthfully what we know and understand. To do this, we need a certain amount of faith. In Buddhism, faith means confidence in our and others' abilities to wake up to our deepest capacity of loving and understanding. In Christianity, faith means trust in God, the One who represents love, understanding, dignity, and truth. When we are still, looking deeply, and touching the source of our true wisdom, we touch the living Buddha and the living Christ in ourselves and in each person we meet.

In this small book, I shall try to share some of my experiences of and insights into two of the world's beautiful flowers, Buddhism and Christianity, so that we as a society can begin to dissolve our wrong perceptions, transcend our wrong views, and see one another in fresh, new ways. If we can enter the twenty-first century with this spirit of mutual understanding and acceptance, our children and their children will surely benefit.

TWO

MINDFULNESS AND

THE HOLY SPIRIT

THE SEED OF THE
HOLY SPIRIT

A year ago in Florence, a Catholic priest told me that he was interested in learning more about Buddhism. I asked him to share with me his understanding of the Holy Spirit and he replied, "The Holy Spirit is the energy sent by God." His statement made me happy. It confirmed my feeling that the

safest way to approach the Trinity is through the
door of the Holy Spirit.

In Buddhism, our effort is to practice mindfulness in each moment—to know what is going on
within and all around us. When the Buddha was
asked, "Sir, what do you and your monks practice?"
he replied, "We sit, we walk, and we eat." The
questioner continued, "But sir, everyone sits, walks,
and eats," and the Buddha told him, "When we sit,
we *know* we are sitting. When we walk, we *know* we
are walking. When we eat, we *know* we are eating."
Most of the time, we are lost in the past or carried
away by future projects and concerns. When we are
mindful, touching deeply the present moment, we
can see and listen deeply, and the fruits are always
understanding, acceptance, love, and the desire to
relieve suffering and bring joy. When our beautiful
child comes up to us and smiles, we are completely
there for her.

To me, mindfulness is very much like the Holy
Spirit. Both are agents of healing. When you have
mindfulness, you have love and understanding, you
see more deeply, and you can heal the wounds in
your own mind. The Buddha was called the King of
Healers. In the Bible, when someone touches
Christ, he or she is healed. It is not just touching a

cloth that brings about a miracle. When you touch deep understanding and love, you are healed.

The Holy Spirit descended on Jesus like a dove, penetrated Him deeply, and He revealed the manifestation of the Holy Spirit. Jesus healed whatever He touched. With the Holy Spirit in Him, His power as a healer transformed many people. All schools of Christianity agree on this. I told the priest that I felt that all of us also have the seed of the Holy Spirit in us, the capacity of healing, transforming, and loving. When we touch that seed, we are able to touch God the Father and God the Son.

∽

PRESENT MOMENT

Touching deeply is an important practice. We touch with our hands, our eyes, our ears, and also with our mindfulness. The first practice I learned as a novice monk was to breathe in and out consciously, to touch each breath with my mindfulness, identifying the in-breath as in-breath and the out-breath as out-breath. When you practice this way, your mind and body come into alignment, your wandering thoughts come to a stop, and you are at your best. Mindfulness is the substance of a Buddha.

When you enter deeply into this moment, you see
the nature of reality, and this insight liberates you
from suffering and confusion. Peace is already there
to some extent: the problem is whether we know
how to touch it. Conscious breathing is the most
basic Buddhist practice for touching peace. I would
like to offer you this short exercise:

Breathing in, I calm my body.
Breathing out, I smile.
Dwelling in the present moment,
I know this is a wonderful moment.

"Breathing in, I calm my body." This is like
drinking a glass of cool water. You feel the freshness
permeate your body. When I breathe in and recite
this line, I actually experience my breathing calming
my body and my mind. In Buddhist meditation,
body and mind become one.

"Breathing out, I smile." One smile can relax
hundreds of muscles in your face and make you
master of yourself. Whenever you see an image of
the Buddha, he is always smiling. When you smile
with mindfulness, you realize the wonder of a
smile.

"Dwelling in the present moment." We recite
this line as we breathe in again, and we don't think

of anything else. We know exactly where we are. Usually we say, "Wait until I finish school and get my Ph.D. degree, and then I will be really alive." But when we obtain it, we say, "I have to wait until I have a job in order to be really alive." After the job, we need a car, and after the car, a house. We are not capable of being alive in the present moment. We always postpone being alive to the future, we don't know exactly when. It is possible we will never be truly alive in our entire life. The technique, if we must speak of a technique, is to *be* in the present moment, to be aware that we are here and now, that the only moment to be alive is the present moment. When we breathe out, we say, "I know this is a wonderful moment." To be truly here, now, and to enjoy the present moment is our most important task.

We can even shorten the verse to six words. As we breathe in, we say to ourselves, "Calming," and as we breathe out, we say, "Smiling." As we breathe in again, we say, "Present moment," and as we breathe out, "Wonderful moment." Practicing this way can help us touch peace right away. We don't have to wait for any other conditions to be present.

Here is another exercise to help us touch peace and serenity:

Breathing in, I am aware of my heart.
Breathing out, I smile to my heart.
I vow to eat, drink, and work in ways
that preserve my health and well-being.

The moment we become truly aware of our heart, we feel comfort and release right away. Our heart has been working day and night, pumping thousands of gallons of blood to nourish all the cells in our body and preserve our peace, and we know that if our heart stops beating, we will die. But still, we do not take good care of our heart. We eat, drink, and work in ways that bring about tension and stress. When we touch our heart with mindfulness, we see clearly that a heart in good condition is an element of real peace and happiness, and we vow to live in a way that keeps our heart in good condition.

❧

MAKING PEACE

We can practice in the same way with our eyes. Our eyes are wonderful, but we usually take them for granted. Every time we open our eyes, we see thousands of marvelous forms and colors. Those who are blind may feel that if they could recover their sight they would be dwelling in paradise, but we who have good eyes rarely take the time to appreciate that we are already in paradise. If we just take a moment to touch our eyes deeply, we will feel real peace and joy.

Touching each part of our body in mindfulness, we make peace with our body, and we can do the same with our feelings. There are many conflicting feelings and ideas within us, and it is important for us to look deeply and know what is going on. When there are wars within us, it will not be long before we are at war with others, even those we love. The violence, hatred, discrimination, and fear in society water the seeds of the violence, hatred, discrimination, and fear in us. If we go back to ourselves and touch our feelings, we will see the ways that we furnish fuel for the wars going on inside. Meditation is, first of all, a tool for surveying our own territory so we can know what is going on. With the energy of mindfulness, we can calm things down, understand them, and bring harmony back to the conflicting elements inside us. If we can learn ways to touch the peace, joy, and happiness that are already there, we will become healthy and strong, and a resource for others.

❧

I AM THERE
FOR YOU

The most precious gift we can offer others is our presence. When our mindfulness embraces those we love, they will bloom like flowers. If you love someone but rarely make yourself available to him or her, that is not true love. When your beloved is suffering, you need to recognize her suffering, anxiety, and worries, and just by doing that, you already offer some relief. Mindfulness relieves suffering because it is filled with understanding and compassion. When you are really there, showing your loving-kindness and understanding, the energy of the Holy Spirit is in you. That is why I told the priest in Florence that mindfulness is very much like the Holy Spirit. Both of them help us touch the ultimate dimension of reality. Mindfulness helps us touch nirvana, and the Holy Spirit offers us a door to the Trinity.

❧

THE LIGHT
THAT REVEALS

When John the Baptist helped Jesus touch the Holy Spirit, the Heavens opened and the Holy

Spirit descended like a dove and entered the person of Jesus. He went to the wilderness and practiced for forty days to strengthen the Spirit in Himself. When mindfulness is born in us, we need to continue to practice if we want it to become solid. Really hearing a bird sing or really seeing a blue sky, we touch the seed of the Holy Spirit within us. Children have little difficulty recognizing the presence of the Holy Spirit. Jesus said that in order to enter the Kingdom of God, we must become like a child. When the energy of the Holy Spirit is in us, we are truly alive, capable of understanding the suffering of others and motivated by the desire to help transform the situation. When the energy of the Holy Spirit is present, God the Father and God the Son are there. That is why I told the priest that touching the Holy Spirit seems to be a safer way to approach the Trinity.

Discussing God is not the best use of our energy. If we touch the Holy Spirit, we touch God not as a concept but as a living reality. In Buddhism, we never talk about nirvana, because nirvana means the extinction of all notions, concepts, and speech. We practice by touching mindfulness in ourselves through sitting meditation, walking meditation, mindful eating, and so on. We observe and learn to handle our body, breathing, feelings, mental states, and consciousness. Living mindfully, shining the

light of our awareness on everything we do, we
touch the Buddha, and our mindfulness grows.

∽

OUR TRUE HOME

The word "Buddha" comes from the root *buddh,*
which means to wake up. A Buddha is someone
who is awake. When Buddhists greet one another,
we hold our palms together like a lotus flower,
breathe in and out mindfully, bow, and say silently,
"A lotus for you, a Buddha to be." This kind of
greeting produces two Buddhas at the same time.
We acknowledge the seeds of awakening, Buddhahood, that are within the other person, whatever his
or her age or status. And we practice mindful
breathing to touch the seed of Buddhahood within
ourselves. Sometimes we can touch the Holy Spirit
or Buddhahood when we are alone, but it is easiest
to practice in a community. That night in Florence I
gave a lecture at that priest's church, and more than
one thousand people came. There was a real feeling
of mutual understanding and community.

A few months later, after attending a retreat in Plum
Village, the community of practice *(Sangha)* where I
live in France, a Catholic priest from North Amer-

ica asked me, "Thây, I see the value of mindfulness practice. I have tasted the joy, peace, and happiness of it. I have enjoyed the bells, the walking, the tea meditation, and the silent meals. But how can I continue to practice when I get back to my church?"

I asked him, "Is there a bell in your church?"

He said, "Yes."

"Do you ring the bell?"

"Yes."

"Then please use your bell as a bell of mindfulness, calling you back to your true home."

When I was a young monk in Vietnam, each village temple had a big bell, like those in Christian churches in Europe and America. Whenever the bell was invited to sound (in Buddhist circles, we never say "hit" or "strike" a bell), all the villagers would stop what they were doing and pause for a few moments to breathe in and out in mindfulness. At Plum Village, every time we hear the bell, we do the same. We go back to ourselves and enjoy our breathing. Breathing in, we say, silently, "Listen, listen," and breathing out, we say, "This wonderful sound brings me back to my true home."

Our true home is in the present moment. The miracle is not to walk on water. The miracle is to walk on the green earth in the present moment. Peace is all around us—in the world and in nature—

and within us—in our bodies and our spirits. Once we learn to touch this peace, we will be healed and transformed. It is not a matter of faith; it is a matter of practice. We need only to bring our body and mind into the present moment, and we will touch what is refreshing, healing, and wondrous.

I asked the priest, "In your church, do you sometimes share a meal? Do you have tea and cookies?"

"Yes."

"Please do it in mindfulness. If you do, there will be no problem at all. When mindfulness is in you, the Holy Spirit is in you, and your friends will see it, not just by what you say, but through your whole being."

THREE

THE FIRST SUPPER

TO BE GRATEFUL

During a conference on religion and peace, a Protestant minister came up to me toward the end of
one of our meals together and said, "Are you a
grateful person?" I was surprised. I was eating
slowly, and I thought to myself, Yes, I am a grateful
person. The minister continued, "If you are really
grateful, how can you not believe in God? God has
created everything we enjoy, including the food we

eat. Since you do not believe in God, you are not grateful for anything." I thought to myself, I feel extremely grateful for everything. Every time I touch food, whenever I see a flower, when I breathe fresh air, I always feel grateful. Why would he say that I am not? I had this incident in mind many years later when I proposed to friends at Plum Village that we celebrate a Buddhist Thanksgiving Day every year. On that day, we practice real gratitude—thanking our mothers, fathers, ancestors, friends, and all beings for everything. If you meet that Protestant minister, I hope you will tell him that we are not ungrateful. We feel deeply grateful for everyone and everything.

Every time we eat a meal, gratitude is our practice. We are grateful for being together as a community. We are grateful that we have food to eat, and we really enjoy the food and the presence of each other. We feel grateful throughout the meal and throughout the day, and we express this by being fully aware of the food and living every moment deeply. This is how I try to express my gratitude to all of life.

∽

LOOKING INTO
OUR FOOD

Mindful eating is an important practice. It nourishes awareness in us. Children are very capable of practicing with us. In Buddhist monasteries, we eat our meals in silence to make it easier to give our full attention to the food and to the other members of the community who are present. And we chew each morsel of food thoroughly, at least thirty times, to help us be truly in touch with it. Eating this way is very good for digestion.

Before every meal, a monk or a nun recites the Five Contemplations: "This food is the gift of the whole universe—the earth, the sky, and much hard work. May we live in a way that is worthy of this food. May we transform our unskillful states of mind, especially that of greed. May we eat only foods that nourish us and prevent illness. May we accept this food for the realization of the way of understanding and love."

Then we can look at the food deeply, in a way that allows it to become real. Contemplating our food before eating in mindfulness can be a real source of happiness. Every time I hold a bowl of rice, I know how fortunate I am. I know that forty thousand children die every day because of the lack of food and that many people are lonely, without friends or family. I visualize them and feel deep compassion. You don't need to be in a monastery to practice this. You can practice at home at your dinner table. Eating mindfully is a wonderful way to nourish compassion, and it encourages us to do something to help those who are hungry and lonely. We needn't be afraid of eating without having the TV, radio, newspaper, or a complicated conversation to distract us. In fact, it is wonderful and joyful to be completely present with our food.

❦

LIVING IN THE PRESENCE OF GOD

In the Jewish tradition, the sacredness of mealtimes is very much emphasized. You cook, set the table, and eat in the presence of God. "Piety" is an important word in Judaism, because all of life is a reflection of God, the infinite source of holiness. The entire world, all the good things in life, belong to God, so when you enjoy something, you think of God and enjoy it in His presence. It is very close to the Buddhist appreciation of interbeing and interpenetration. When you wake up, you are aware that

God created the world. When you see rays of sunlight streaming through your window, you recognize the presence of God. When you stand up and your feet touch the ground, you know the earth belongs to God. When you wash your face, you know that the water is God. Piety is the recognition that everything is linked to the presence of God in every moment. The Passover Seder, for example, is a ritual meal to celebrate the freedom of the Israelites from bondage in Egypt and their journey home. During the meal, certain vegetables and herbs, salt, and other condiments help us touch what happened in the past—what was our suffering and what was our hope. This is a practice of mindfulness.

∞

THE BREAD WE EAT IS
THE WHOLE COSMOS

Christianity is a kind of continuation of Judaism, as is Islam. All the branches belong to the same tree. In Christianity, when we celebrate the Eucharist, sharing the bread and the wine as the body of God, we do it in the same spirit of piety, of mindfulness, aware that we are alive, enjoying dwelling in the present moment. The message of Jesus during the Seder that has become known as the Last Supper was clear. His disciples had been following Him. They had had the chance to look in His eyes and see Him in person, but it seems they had not yet come into real contact with the marvelous reality of His being. So when Jesus broke the bread and poured the wine, he said, This is My body. This is My blood. Drink it, eat it, and you will have life eternal. It was a drastic way to awaken His disciples from forgetfulness.

When we look around, we see many people in whom the Holy Spirit does not appear to dwell. They look dead, as though they were dragging around a corpse, their own body. The practice of the Eucharist is to help resurrect these people so they can touch the Kingdom of Life. In the church, the Eucharist is received at every mass. Representatives of the church read from the biblical passage about the Last Supper of Jesus with His twelve disciples, and a special kind of bread called the Host is shared. Everyone partakes as a way to receive the life of Christ into his or her own body. When a priest performs the Eucharistic rite, his role is to bring life to the community. The miracle happens not because he says the words correctly, but because we eat and drink in mindfulness. Holy Communion is a strong bell of mindfulness. We drink and eat all the time, but we usually ingest only our ideas, projects, worries, and anxiety. We do not really eat our bread or drink our beverage. If we allow ourselves to touch our bread deeply, we become reborn, because our bread is life itself. Eating it deeply, we touch the sun, the clouds, the earth, and everything in the cosmos. We touch life, and we touch the Kingdom of God. When I asked Cardinal Jean Daniélou if the Eucharist can be described in this way, he said yes.

∽

THE BODY OF
REALITY

It is ironic that when mass is said today, many congregants are not called to mindfulness at all. They have heard the words so many times that they just feel a little distracted. This is exactly what Jesus was trying to overcome when he said, This is My body. This is My blood. When we are truly there, dwelling deeply in the present moment, we can see that the bread and the wine are really the Body and Blood of Christ and the priest's words are truly the words of the Lord. The body of Christ is the body of God, the body of ultimate reality, the ground of all existence. We do not have to look anywhere else for it. It resides deep in our own being. The Eucharistic rite encourages us to be fully aware so that we can touch the body of reality in us. Bread and wine are not symbols. They contain the reality, just as we do.

❧

EVERYTHING IS
FRESH AND NEW

When Buddhists and Christians come together, we should share a meal in mindfulness as a deep practice of Communion. When we pick up a piece of bread, we can do it with mindfulness, with Spirit. The bread, the Host, becomes the object of our deep love and concentration. If our concentration is not strong enough, we can try saying its name silently, "Bread," in the way we would call the name of our beloved. When we do this, the bread will reveal itself to us in its totality, and we can put it in our mouth and chew with real awareness, not chewing anything else, such as our thoughts, our fears, or even our aspirations. This is Holy Communion, to live in faith. When we practice this way, every meal is the Last Supper. In fact, we could call it the First Supper, because everything will be fresh and new.

When we eat together in this way, the food and the community of co-practitioners are the objects of our mindfulness. It is through the food and one another that the ultimate becomes present. To eat a piece of bread or a bowl of rice mindfully and see that every morsel is a gift of the whole universe is to live deeply. We do not need to distract ourselves from the food, even by listening to scriptures or the lives of bodhisattvas or saints. When mindfulness is present, the Buddha and the Holy Spirit are already there.

FOUR

LIVING BUDDHA,

LIVING CHRIST

HIS LIFE IS
HIS TEACHING

There is a science called Buddhology, the study of the life of the Buddha. As an historical person, the Buddha was born in Kapilavastu, near the border between India and Nepal, got married, had one child, left home, practiced many kinds of meditation, became enlightened, and shared the teaching until he died at the age of eighty. But there is also the Buddha within ourselves who transcends space and time. This is the living Buddha, the Buddha of the ultimate reality, the one who transcends all ideas and notions and is available to us at any time. The living Buddha was not born at Kapilavastu, nor did he pass away at Kushinagar.

Christology is the study of the life of Christ. When speaking about Christ, we also have to know whether we mean the historical Jesus or the living Jesus. The historical Jesus was born in Bethlehem, the son of a carpenter, traveled far from his homeland, became a teacher, and was crucified at the age of thirty-three. The living Jesus is the Son of God who was resurrected and who continues to live. In Christianity, you have to believe in the resurrection or you are not considered a Christian. I am afraid this criterion may discourage some people from looking into the life of Jesus. That is a pity, because we can appreciate Jesus Christ as both an historical door and an ultimate door.

When we look into and touch deeply the life and teaching of Jesus, we can penetrate the reality of God. Love, understanding, courage, and acceptance are expressions of the life of Jesus. God made Himself known to us through Jesus Christ. With the Holy Spirit and the Kingdom of God within Him, Jesus touched the people of his time. He talked with prostitutes and tax collectors, and had the courage to do whatever was needed to heal His society. As the child of Mary and Joseph, Jesus is the Son of Woman and Man. As someone animated by the energy of the Holy Spirit, He is the Son of God. The fact that Jesus is both the Son of Man and the Son of God is not difficult for a Buddhist to accept. We can see the nature of nonduality in God the Son and God the Father, because without God the Father within Him, the Son could never be. But in Christianity, Jesus is usually seen as the only Son of God. I think it is important to look deeply into every act and every teaching of Jesus during His lifetime, and to use this as a model for our own practice. Jesus lived exactly as He taught, so studying the life of Jesus is crucial to understanding His teaching. For me, the life of Jesus is His most basic teaching, more important than even faith in the resurrection or faith in eternity.

❧

MINDFULNESS IS THE BUDDHA

The Buddha was a human being who was awakened and, thereby, no longer bound by the many afflictions of life. But when some Buddhists say that they believe in the Buddha, they are expressing their faith in the wonderful, universal Buddhas, not in the teaching or the life of the historical Buddha. They believe in the Buddha's magnificence and feel that is enough. But the examples of the actual lives of the Buddha and of Jesus are most important, because as human beings, they lived in ways that we can live, too.

When we read, "The heavens opened and the Holy Spirit descended upon Him like a dove," we can see that Jesus Christ was already enlightened. He was in touch with the reality of life, the source of mindfulness, wisdom, and understanding within Him, and this made Him different from other human beings. When He was born into a carpenter's family, He was the Son of Man. When He opened His heart, the door of Heaven was opened to Him. The Holy Spirit descended on Him like a dove, and He was manifested as the Son of God—very holy, very deep, and very great. But the Holy Spirit is not just for Jesus alone; it is for all of us. From a Buddhist perspective, who is not the son or daughter of God? Sitting beneath the Bodhi tree, many wonderful, holy seeds within the Buddha blossomed forth. He was human, but, at the same time, he became an expression of the highest spirit of humanity. *When we are in touch with the highest spirit in ourselves, we too are a Buddha, filled with the Holy Spirit, and we become very tolerant, very open, very deep, and very understanding.*

∽

MORE DOORS FOR
FUTURE GENERATIONS

Matthew described the Kingdom of God as being like a tiny mustard seed. It means that the seed of the Kingdom of God is within us. If we know how to plant that seed in the moist soil of our daily lives, it will grow and become a large bush on which many birds can take refuge. We do not have to die to arrive at the gates of Heaven. In fact, we have to be truly alive. The practice is to touch life deeply so that the Kingdom of God becomes a reality. This is not a matter of devotion. It is a matter of practice. The Kingdom of God is available here and now. Many passages in the Gospels support this view. We read in The Lord's Prayer that we do not *go* to the Kingdom of God, but the Kingdom of God comes to us: "Thy Kingdom come . . ." Jesus said, "I am the door." He describes Himself as the door of salvation and everlasting life, the door to the Kingdom of God. Because God the Son is made of the energy of the Holy Spirit, He is the door for us to enter the Kingdom of God.

The Buddha is also described as a door, a teacher who shows us the way in this life. In Buddhism such a special door is deeply appreciated because that door allows us to enter the realm of mindfulness, loving-kindness, peace, and joy. But it is said that there are 84,000 *Dharma* doors, doors of teaching. If you are lucky enough to find a door, it would not be very Buddhist to say that yours is the only door. In fact, we have to open even more doors for future generations. We should not be afraid of more Dharma doors—if anything, we should be afraid that no more will be opened. It would be a pity for our children and their children if we were satisfied with only the 84,000 doors already available. Each of us, by our practice and our loving-kindness, is capable of opening new Dharma doors. Society is changing, people are changing, economic and political conditions are not the same as they were in the time of the Buddha or Jesus. The Buddha relies on us for the Dharma to continue to develop as a living organism—not a stale Dharma, but a real *Dharmakaya,* a real "body of teaching."

⚭

THE MOTHER OF
ALL BUDDHAS

The Buddha said that his Dharma body is more important than his physical body. He meant that we have to practice the Dharma in order to make nirvana available here and now. The living Dharma is not a library of scriptures or tapes of inspiring lectures. The living Dharma is mindfulness, manifested in the Buddha's daily life and in your daily life, also. When I see you walking mindfully, I touch the peace, joy, and deep presence of your being. When you take good care of your brothers and sisters, I recognize the living Dharma in you. If you are mindful, the Dharmakaya is easy to touch.

The Buddha described the seed of mindfulness that is in each of us as the "womb of the Buddha" *(tathagatagarbha)*. We are all mothers of the Buddha because we are all pregnant with the potential for awakening. If we know how to take care of our baby Buddha by practicing mindfulness in our daily lives, one day the Enlightened One will reveal himself or herself to us. Buddhists regard the Buddha as a teacher and a brother, not as a god. We are all Dharma brothers and sisters of the Buddha. We also say that *Prajñaparamita* (Perfection of Wisdom) is the mother of all Buddhas. Historically, in Protestantism, the feminine side of God has been minimized and God the Father has been emphasized, but in Catholicism, there is a great deal of devotion to Mary, the Mother of God. In fact, "father" and "mother" are two aspects of the same reality. Father is more expressive of the side of wisdom or understanding, and mother the side of love or compassion. In Buddhism, understanding *(prajña)* is essential to love *(maitri)*. Without understanding there cannot be true love, and without love there cannot be true understanding.

∽

THE DAUGHTER
OF GOD

The Buddha is said to have ten names, each describing an auspicious quality. The first, *Tathagata,* means "he who has come to us through the right path," "he who comes from the wonderful reality of life and will go back to that wonderful reality," and "he who has arrived from suchness, remains in suchness, and will return to suchness." "Suchness" is a Buddhist term pointing to the true nature of things, or ultimate reality. It is the substance or ground of being, just as water is the substance of waves. Like the Buddha, we too have come from suchness, remain in suchness, and will return to suchness. We have come from nowhere and have nowhere to go.

One Buddhist sutra tells us that when conditions are sufficient, we see forms, and when conditions are not sufficient, we don't. When all conditions are present, phenomena can be perceived by us, and so they are revealed to us as existing. But when one of these conditions is lacking, we cannot perceive the same phenomena, so they are not revealed to us, and we say they do not exist. But that is not true. In April, for example, we cannot see sunflowers around Plum Village, our community in southwestern France, so you might say the sunflowers do not exist. But the local farmers have already planted thousands of seeds, and when they look at the bare hills, they see sunflowers already. The sunflowers *are there*. They lack only the conditions of sun, heat, rain, and July. Just because you cannot see them does not mean that they do not exist. In the same way we say that the Tathagatha does not come from anywhere and will not go anywhere. He comes from ultimate reality and will go back to ultimate reality, unbound by space and time. If you walk past the fields near Plum Village in April and ask them to reveal to you the ultimate dimension of reality, the Kingdom of God, the fields will suddenly be covered with beautiful, golden sunflowers. When St. Francis looked deeply at an almond tree in winter and asked it to speak to him about God, the tree was instantly covered with blossoms.

The second name of the Buddha is *Arhat,* "one who is worthy of our respect and support." The third is *Samyaksambuddha,* "one who is perfectly enlightened." The fourth is *Vidyacaranasampana,* "one who is endowed with insight and conduct." The fifth is *Sugata,* "one who has gone happily along the path." The sixth is *Lokavidu,* "one who knows the world well." The seventh is *Anuttarapurusadamyasarathi,* "the unsurpassed leader of those to be trained and taught." The eighth is *Sastadevamanusyanam,* "teacher of gods and humans." The ninth is *Buddha,* "enlightened one." The tenth is *Bhagavat,* "blessed one." Every time we take refuge in the Buddha, we take refuge in the one who has these ten attributes, which are at the core of human nature. Siddhartha is not the only Buddha. All beings in the animal, plant, and mineral worlds are potential Buddhas. We all contain these ten qualities of a Buddha in the core of our being. If we can realize these qualities in ourselves, we will be respected and honored by all people.

I see the rite of Baptism as a way of recognizing that every human being, when opened to the Holy Spirit, is capable of manifesting these qualities, which are also the qualities of being a son or daughter of God. We do not speak about Original Sin in Buddhism, but we do talk about negative seeds that exist in every person—seeds of hatred, anger, ignorance, intolerance, and so on—and we say that these seeds can be transformed when we touch the qualities of a Buddha, which are also seeds within us. Original sin can be transformed when one is in touch with the Holy Spirit. Jesus is the Son of God and the Son of Man. We are all, at the same time, the sons and daughters of God and the children of our parents. This means we are of the same reality as Jesus. This may sound heretical to many Christians, but I believe that theologians who say we are not have to reconsider this. Jesus is not only our Lord, but He is also our Father, our Teacher, our Brother, and our Self. The only place we can touch Jesus and the Kingdom of God is within us.

~

WE CONTINUE
TO BE BORN

When we celebrate Christmas or the birth of the Buddha, we celebrate the coming into the world of a very special child. The births of Jesus and the Buddha were pivotal events in human history. A few days after the Buddha was born, many people in his country of Kapilavastu came to pay their respects, including an old sage named Asita. After contemplating the baby Buddha, Asita began to cry. The king, the Buddha's father, was alarmed. "Holy man, why are you crying? Will some misfortune overtake my child?" The holy man replied, "No, your majesty. The birth of Prince Siddhartha is a wondrous event. Your child will become an important world teacher. But I am too old and I will not be there. That is the only reason I am crying."

A similar story appears in the Bible. Eight days after His birth, the baby Jesus was brought to the temple for circumcision. When a man named Simeon looked at Him, he was able to see that Jesus would bring about a profound change in the life of humankind: "When the time came for the purification according to the law of Moses, they brought him up to Jerusalem to present him to the Lord

. . . and they offered a sacrifice according to what
is stated in the law of the Lord, a pair of turtle doves,
or two young pigeons. Now there was a man in
Jerusalem whose name was Simeon. This man was
righteous and devout, looking forward to the conso-
lation of Israel, and the Holy Spirit rested on him. It
had been revealed to him by the Holy Spirit that he
would not see death before he had seen the Lord's
Messiah. Guided by the spirit, Simeon came into the
temple and when the parents brought in the child
Jesus to do for him what was customary under the
law, Simeon took him in his arms and praised God,
saying, 'Master, now you are dismissing your servant
in peace according to your word, for my eyes have
seen your salvation which you have prepared in the
presence of all peoples, a light for revelation to the
gentiles and for glory to your people, Israel.' And
the child's father and mother were amazed at what
was being said about him."

Whenever I read the stories of Asita and Simeon,
I have the wish that every one of us could have been
visited by a sage when we were born. The birth of
every child is important, not less than the birth of a
Buddha. We, too, are a Buddha, a Buddha-to-be,
and we continue to be born every minute. We, too,
are sons and daughters of God and the children of

our parents. We have to take special care of each birth.

∽

TOUCHING OUR
ANCESTORS

I am not sure if I am myself or if I am my brother. Before I came into the world, another boy tried to come before me, but my mother miscarried him. If he had continued to live, I would have another brother. Or perhaps I would have been my brother. Many times as a child, I pondered this.

Expecting parents have to be very careful because they carry within them a baby, one who might become a Buddha or Lord Jesus. They have to be mindful of what they eat, what they drink, what they think, and how they act. The way they take care of their bodies and their feelings affects the well-being of the child within. Our mothers and fathers helped us come to be and, even now, they continue to give us life. Whenever I have difficulties, I ask for their support, and they always respond.

Our spiritual ancestors have also given birth to us, and they, too, continue to give birth to us. In my country, we say that an authentic teacher has the power to give birth to a disciple. If you have enough spiritual strength, you will give birth to a spiritual child, and through your life and practice, you continue giving birth, even after you die. We say that sons and daughters of the Buddha came forth from the mouth of the Buddha, because the Buddha offered them the Dharma, his teachings. There are many ways to offer the Dharma for a child to be born in his or her spiritual life, but the most usual is to share the Dharma through words. I try to practice in a way that allows me to touch my blood ancestors and my spiritual ancestors every day. Whenever I feel sad or a little fragile, I invoke their presence for support, and they never fail to be there.

∞

SUFFERING AND
THE WAY OUT

As children, Siddhartha and Jesus both realized that life is filled with suffering. The Buddha became aware at an early age that suffering is pervasive. Jesus must have had the same kind of insight, because they both made every effort to offer a way out. We, too, must learn to live in ways that reduce the world's suffering. Suffering is always there, around us and inside us, and we have to find ways that alleviate the suffering and transform it into well-being and peace.

Monks and nuns in both their traditions practice prayer, meditation, mindful walking, silent meals, and many other ways to try to overcome suffering. It is a kind of luxury to be a monk or a nun, to be able to sit quietly and look deeply into the nature of suffering and the way out. Sitting and looking deeply into your body, your consciousness, and your mental states is like being a mother hen covering her eggs. One day insight will be born like a baby chick. If monks and nuns do not cherish their time of practice, they will have nothing to offer to the world.

The Buddha was twenty-nine, quite young, when he became a monk, and at the age of thirty-five, he was enlightened. Jesus also spent time alone on the mountain and in the desert. We all need time to reflect and to refresh ourselves. For those who are not monks or nuns, it may be difficult to find the time to meditate or pray, but it is important to do so. During a retreat, we learn how to maintain awareness of each thing we do, and then we can continue the practice in our daily lives. If we do this, we will see deeply into the nature of our suffering, and we will find a way out. That is what the Buddha said in his first Dharma talk at the Deer Park in Sarnath: "Look deeply into the nature of suffering to see the causes of suffering and the way out." Monks and non-monks can all practice this.

∽

I AM THE WAY

The Theravada school of Buddhism emphasizes the actual teaching of the historical Buddha, the Buddha who lived and died. Later, the idea of the living Buddha was developed in the Buddhism of the Northern schools, the Mahayana. When the Buddha was about to pass away, many of his disciples were upset that he would no longer be with them. So he reassured them by saying, "My physical body will no longer be here, but my teaching body, Dharmakaya, will always be with you. Take refuge in the Dharma, the teaching, to make an island for yourselves." The Buddha's instructions are clear. The Dharma is our island of refuge, the torch lighting our path. If we have the teaching, we needn't worry. One monk who was very ill expressed regret at not being able to see the Buddha in person, but the Buddha sent word to him: "My physical body is not what is most important. If you have the Dharma body with you, if you have confidence in the Dharma, if you practice the Dharma, I am always with you." Jesus also said, "Whenever two or three are gathered in my name, I am there."

≈

I AM ALWAYS
THERE FOR YOU

After the Buddha passed away, the love and devotion to him became so great that the idea of Dharmakaya changed from the body of teaching to the glorious, eternal Buddha, who is always expounding the Dharma. According to Mahayana Buddhism, the Buddha is still alive, continuing to give Dharma talks. If you are attentive enough, you will be able to hear his teachings from the voice of a pebble, a leaf, or a cloud in the sky. The enduring Buddha has become the living Buddha, the Buddha of faith. This is very much like the Christ of faith, the living Christ. Protestant theologian Paul Tillich describes God as the ground of being. The Buddha is also sometimes described as the ground of being.

∞

SEEING THE WAY
IS SEEING ME

To encounter a true master is said to be worth a century of studying his or her teaching, because in such a person we witness a living example of enlightenment. How can we encounter Jesus or the Buddha? It depends on us. Many who looked directly into the eyes of the Buddha or Jesus were not capable of seeing them. One man who wanted to see the Buddha was in such a hurry that he neglected a woman in dire need whom he met along the way. When he arrived at the Buddha's monastery, he was incapable of seeing him. Whether you can see the Buddha or not depends on you, on the state of your being.

∞

I AM UNDERSTANDING,
I AM LOVE

Like many great humans, the Buddha had a hallowed presence. When we see such persons, we feel peace, love, and strength in them, and also in ourselves. The Chinese say, "When a sage is born, the river water becomes clearer and the mountain plants and trees become more verdant." They are describing the ambience surrounding a holy man or woman. When a sage is present and you sit near him or her, you feel peace and light. If you were to sit close to Jesus and look into His eyes—even if you didn't see Him—you would have a much greater chance to be saved than by reading His words. But when He is not there, His teachings are second best, especially the teachings of His life.

∽

FREEDOM FROM NOTIONS

When I read any scripture, Christian or Buddhist, I always keep in mind that whatever Jesus or the Buddha said was to a particular person or group on a particular occasion. I try to understand deeply the context in which they spoke in order to really understand their meaning. What they said may be less important than how they said it. When we understand this, we are close to Jesus or the Buddha. But if we analyze their words to find the deepest meaning without understanding the relationships between the speaker and his listeners, we may miss the point. Theologians sometimes forget this.

When we read the Bible, we see Jesus' tremen-

dous courage in trying to transform the life of His
society. When we read the sutras, we see that the
Buddha was also a very strong person. The society
of India at the time of the Buddha was less violent
than the society into which Jesus was born, so you
may think the Buddha was less extreme in his reac-
tions, but that is only because another way was possible in his milieu. His reaction to the corruption
among Vedic priests, for example, was thorough-
going. The notion of *Atman,* Self, which was at the
center of Vedic beliefs, was the cause of much of the
social injustice of the day—the caste system, the terrible treatment of the untouchables, and the monop-
olization of spiritual teachings by those who enjoyed
the best material conditions and yet were hardly
spiritual at all. In reaction, the Buddha emphasized
the teachings of non-Atman (non-self). He said,
"Things are empty of a separate, independent self. If
you look for the self of a flower, you will see that it
is empty." But when Buddhists began worshiping
the idea of emptiness, he said, "It is worse if you get
caught in the non-self of a flower than if you believe
in the self of a flower."

The Buddha did not present an absolute doctrine. His teaching of non-self was offered in the
context of his time. It was an instrument for meditation. But many Buddhists since then have gotten

caught by the idea of non-self. They confuse the means and the end, the raft and the shore, the finger pointing to the moon and the moon. There is something more important than non-self. It is the freedom from the notions of both self and non-self. For a Buddhist to be attached to any doctrine, even a Buddhist one, is to betray the Buddha. It is not words or concepts that are important. What is important is our insight into the nature of reality and our way of responding to reality. If the Buddha had been born into the society in which Jesus was born, I think he, too, would have been crucified.

∞

SEEING THE WAY,
TAKING THE PATH

When Jesus said, "I am the way," He meant that to have a true relationship with God, you must practice His way. In the Acts of the Apostles, the early Christians always spoke of their faith as "the Way." To me, "I am the way" is a better statement than "I know the way." The way is not an asphalt road. But we must distinguish between the "I" spoken by Jesus and the "I" that people usually think of. The "I" in His statement is *life* itself, His life, which is the way. If you do not really look at His life, you cannot see the way. If you only satisfy yourself with praising a name, even the *name* of Jesus, it is not practicing the life of Jesus. We must practice living deeply, loving, and acting with charity if we wish to truly honor Jesus. The way is Jesus Himself and not just some idea of Him. A true teaching is not static. It is not mere words but the reality of life. Many who have neither the way nor the life try to impose on others what they believe to be the way. But these are only words that have no connection with real life or a real way. *When we understand and practice deeply the life and teachings of Buddha or the life and teachings of Jesus, we penetrate the door and enter the abode of the living Buddha and the living Christ, and life eternal presents itself to us.*

∞

YOUR BODY IS THE
BODY OF CHRIST

When the Protestant minister described me as someone who is not grateful, he was speaking a language different from Buddhism. To him, love could only be symbolized by a person. That is why belief in the resurrection is so important to Christians. If Jesus died and was not resurrected, who would carry His eternal love for us? But does God have to be personified? In Judaism and Christianity, the image of a person is always used.

In Buddhism, we also personify traits we aspire toward, such as mindfulness (Shakyamuni Buddha), understanding (Manjusri Bodhisattva), and love (Maitreya Buddha), but even if Shakyamuni, Manjusri, and Maitreya are not there, it is still possible to touch mindfulness, understanding, and love. Students of the Buddha are themselves a continuation of the Buddha. It is possible to manifest mindfulness, understanding, and love through people of our own time, even ourselves. We do not need to believe in the resurrection of Buddhas and bodhisattvas as much as in producing mindfulness, understanding, and love in ourselves.

The living Christ is the Christ of Love who is always generating love, moment after moment. When the church manifests understanding, tolerance, and loving-kindness, Jesus is there. Christians have to help Jesus Christ be manifested by their way of life, showing those around them that love, understanding, and tolerance are possible. This will not be accomplished just by books and sermons. It has to be realized by the way we live. In Buddhism we also say the living Buddha, the one who teaches love and compassion, must be manifested by the way we live.

Thanks to the practice of many generations of

Buddhists and Christians, the energy of the Buddha and the energy of Jesus Christ have come to us. We can touch the living Buddha and we can touch the living Christ. We know that our body is the continuation of the Buddha's body and is a member of the mystical body of Christ. We have a wonderful opportunity to help the Buddha and Jesus Christ continue. Thanks to our bodies and our lives, the practice is possible. If you hate your body and think that it is only a source of affliction, that it contains only the roots of anger, hatred, and craving, you do not understand that your body is the body of the Buddha, your body is a member of the body of Christ.

∾

ENJOY BEING ALIVE

To breathe and know you are alive is wonderful. Because you are alive, everything is possible. The Sangha, the community of practice, can continue. The church can continue. Please don't waste a single moment. Every moment is an opportunity to breathe life into the Buddha, the Dharma, and the Sangha. Every moment is an opportunity to manifest the Father, the Son, and the Holy Spirit.

"There is a person whose appearance on earth is for the well-being and happiness of all. Who is that person?" This is a question from the *Anguttara Nikaya.* For Buddhists, that person is the Buddha. For Christians, that person is Jesus Christ. Through your daily life, you can help that person continue. You only need to walk in mindfulness, making peaceful, happy steps on our planet. Breathe deeply, and enjoy your breathing. Be aware that the sky is blue and the birds' songs are beautiful. Enjoy being alive and you will help the living Christ and the living Buddha continue for a long, long time.

FIVE

COMMUNITIES OF

PRACTICE

MINDFULNESS OF WORKING

St. Gregory of Nyssa taught that the contemplative life is heavenly and cannot be lived in the world, that whenever a monk has to leave the monastery to do some apostolic work, he must lament. Many monks do in fact cry when they have to leave their monasteries for an apostolic ministry. Other teachers, like St. Basil, said that it is possible to pray as you work. But he did not mean that we can pray with our actions. He meant pray with our mouths and our hearts. In Vietnam, we invented "engaged Buddhism" so we could continue our contemplative life while in the midst of helping the victims of war. There must be ways for monks to continue their contemplative lives while engaging in society. In Vietnam, we did not try to avoid the suffering. We worked to relieve the suffering while, at the same time, trying to maintain our mindfulness.

Even in monasteries, we have to cook, clean, sweep, and wash. How can we avoid these? Is there a way to work in a meditative mood? The answer is clearly yes. We practice mindfulness of cooking, cleaning, sweeping, and washing. When we work this way, we touch the ultimate dimension of reality. But we need training to do this, and it helps very much to have a community in which all the members are sharing the same practice. In fact, it is crucial to be with a Sangha or a church where everyone practices together, or dwells mindfully in the Spirit. We need to create such communities for our own benefit.

❧

MONASTIC CULTURE

Thomas Merton wrote about monastic culture. A monastery or practice center is a place where insight is transformed into action. The monastery should be an expression of our insight, our peace, and our joy, a place where peace and beauty are possible. The way the monks and nuns there walk, eat, and work expresses their insight and their joy.

When someone from the city arrives in a monastery compound, just seeing the trees and gardens and hearing the sounds of the bell can calm him down. When he meets a monk walking peacefully, his tension may wash away. The environment, the sights, and the sounds of the monastery begin to work in him for healing and transformation, even before he listens to any liturgy or teaching. Through their true practice and genuine insight, those who live in monasteries, temples, and practice centers offer us a way to obtain peace, joy, and freedom.

When monks offer retreats, they initiate people into the practice of mindfulness, of touching the best things within themselves and touching the ultimate dimension. They know the time is limited, so they offer only practices that retreatants can bring home and continue in their daily lives. If someone is too busy for a week-long retreat, it is still helpful to come for a weekend or a day of mindfulness, or even half a day. The monks and nuns can offer the peace, joy, and stability they have obtained through the practice. This kind of life can be described as monastic culture.

When you practice with others, it is much easier to obtain stability, joy, and freedom. If you have a chance to visit a retreat center, I hope you enjoy your time there sitting, walking, breathing, praying, and doing everything in mindfulness. The seeds are being watered, and the fruit, transformation, will reveal itself.

≫

COMMUNITY AS A REFUGE

In Christianity, the church is the crown of the path of practice, the true teaching authority. It is often said that there is no salvation outside the church. In Buddhism, a Sangha is a group of monks, nuns, laymen, and laywomen who practice together to encourage the best qualities in each other. Some Buddhists respect only the Holy Sangha, the actual disciples of the Buddha during his lifetime. But they are already gone. To me, to practice with the Sangha

means to practice with those who are with you now
and with those you love. It may not be a Holy Sangha, but if it moves in the direction of transformation, it is a real Sangha. We do not need a perfect or
a Holy Sangha to practice. An imperfect Sangha is
good enough. We can help build and improve the
Sangha by practicing mindfully, step by step, encouraging each other. There is a saying: If a tiger
comes down off his mountain and goes to the low-
lands, he will be caught by humans and killed. It
means if a practitioner leaves his or her Sangha, it
becomes difficult to continue the practice. Taking
refuge in the Sangha is not a matter of devotion. It is
a matter of practice. The Buddhist Sangha includes
Arhats, those who have overcome all afflictions, and
Stream-enterers, those who have entered the stream
that will surely lead them to enlightenment. Stream-
enterers have no doubt that the practice will transform their suffering. In Christianity, some people
have been declared saints or holy persons. Perhaps
they are similar to Arhats and Stream-enterers, but I
must confess I don't understand how it is decided
who is a saint.

∾

COMMUNITY AS A
BODY

In John 15, Jesus says, "I am the true vine . . .
Abide in me as I abide in you. Just as the branch
cannot bear fruit by itself unless it abides in the vine,
neither can you unless you abide in me." This is
close to Buddhism. Without mindfulness, we cannot
bear the fruit of love, understanding, and liberation.
We must bring forth the Buddha in ourselves. We
have to evoke the living Buddha in ourselves in order to become more understanding and more loving. Jesus said, "Wherever two or three are gathered
in My name, there I am." In Buddhism, it takes at
least four persons practicing together to be called a
Sangha. That allows the Sanghakarma, the legal pro-
cedure for making decisions in community life, to
be possible.

When we live as a Sangha, we regard each other
as brothers and sisters, and we practice the Six Con-
cords—sharing space, sharing the essentials of daily
life, observing the same precepts, using only words
that contribute to harmony, sharing our insights and
understanding, and respecting each other's viewpoints. A community that follows these principles
always lives happily and at peace.

When we gather together to form a Sangha, we practice opening up the confines of our separate self and become a large body of love and understanding. We and our brothers and sisters are one. This idea of salvation is echoed in the Eastern Orthodox church, which has even more of a sense of togetherness— you can only be saved as a community.

∽

THE HOLY SPIRIT IS THE SOUL OF THE CHURCH

When you hammer a nail into a board and accidentally strike your finger, you take care of the injury immediately. The right hand never says to the left hand, "I am doing charitable work for you." It just does whatever it can to help—giving first aid, compassion, and concern. In the Mahayana Buddhist tradition, the practice of *dana,* generosity, is like this. We do whatever we can to benefit others without seeing ourselves as helpers and the others as the helped. This is the spirit of non-self.

In Christianity, every member of the church is said to be a part of the body of Christ. In Buddhism, we say that each Sangha member is like a hand or a leg of the Buddha. When we live in accord with the teachings of the Buddha, we are members of one body. If we practice the precepts well and realize deep concentration and understanding, our Sangha can arrive at liberation from afflictions. Even when liberation is not yet total, people can look at our community and appreciate the loving and harmonious atmosphere. When we practice understanding and love, we are a real Sangha, a fertile field in which good seeds will surely flower.

If there are too many misunderstandings, disputes, and rivalries among members, a Sangha cannot be called a real Sangha, even if it is in a beautiful temple or famous practice center. A church or community that is not filled with the Holy Spirit is not alive. A Sangha that is not pervaded by the energy of mindfulness is not authentic. For a community to be a real place of practice or worship, its members have to cultivate mindfulness, understanding, and love. A church where people are unkind to each other or suppress each other is not a true church. The Holy Spirit is not there. If you want to renew your church, bring the energy of the Holy Spirit into it. When people appreciate each other as brothers and sisters and smile, the Holy Spirit is there. When mindfulness is present, understanding *(prajña)* and love *(maitri* and *karuna)* are there, also.

∞

THE HOLY SPIRIT IS THE
ENERGY OF LOVE AND
UNDERSTANDING

To have a good Sangha, the members must live in a way that helps them generate more understanding and more love. If a Sangha is having difficulties, the way to transform it is to begin by transforming yourself, to go back to your island of self and become more refreshed and more understanding. You will be like the first candle that lights the second that lights the third, fourth, and fifth. But if you try your best to practice in this way and the people in the community still have no light, it may be necessary to find another Sangha or even start a new one. But don't give up too easily. Perhaps you have not practiced deeply enough to transform yourself into a living candle capable of lighting all the other candles. Only when you are convinced that creating a new Sangha is the only alternative to giving up is it time to go ahead and create a new Sangha. Any Sangha is better than a non-Sangha. Without a Sangha, you will be lost.

The same is true within a church. If you see that the Holy Spirit is not present in your church, first make the effort to bring the Holy Spirit in by living deeply the teachings of Jesus. But if you have no impact, if the practice in the church is not in accord with the life and teachings of Jesus, you may wish to gather those who share your conviction and set up another church, where you can invite the Holy Spirit to enter. To be a real help to your church or Sangha, you must first light your own fire of understanding, love, solidity, and stillness. Then you will be able to inspire others, whether in an existing group or one you are helping establish. Please don't practice "religious imperialism." Even if you have a beautiful temple or church with fine decorations and artwork, if inside there is no tolerance, happiness, understanding, or love, it is a false Sangha, a false church. Please continue to make an effort to do better.

∽

TO BE REAL
SALT

The living teaching expressed by the lives of the Buddha and Jesus should always be the models for our practice. The sutras are not the living teachings of the Buddha. To receive the true teaching, we must emulate the life and work of the Buddha himself. The same is true of Christianity. The Gospels in their written or even oral form are not the living teaching of Jesus. The teachings *must be practiced* as they were lived by Jesus.

The church is the vehicle that allows us to realize those teachings. The church is the hope of Jesus, just as the Sangha is the hope of the Buddha. It is through the practice of the church and the Sangha that the teachings come alive. Communities of practice, with all their shortcomings, are the best way to make the teachings available to people. The Father, Son and the Holy Spirit need the church in order to be manifested. ("Wherever two or three are gathered in My Name, there I am.") People can touch the Father and the Son through the church. That is why we say that the church is the mystical body of Christ. Jesus was very clear about the need to practice the teaching and to do so in community. He told His disciples to be the light of the world. For a Buddhist, that means mindfulness. The Buddha said that we must each be our own torch. Jesus also told His disciples to be the salt of the world, to be real salt. His teaching was clear and strong. If the church practices well the teachings of Jesus, the Trinity will always be present and the church will have a healing power to transform all that it touches.

∞

ARE WE PRACTICING
THE TRUE TEACHING?

Are we making Jesus' presence real in our churches today? Are we making the Buddha's presence real in our Sanghas? The Buddha and the monks and nuns of his time were in continuous dialogue with those of other religious faiths, especially the Brahmans. Are we in dialogue with other religions? The Buddha made every effort to remove the barriers between classes. He accepted untouchables and other outcasts into his holy community. Are we doing the same with the poor and oppressed of our day? Are we bringing the service of the Sangha and the church to those who suffer, to those who are discriminated against politically, racially, and economically?

The Buddha accepted women into his Sangha and they became teachers, transmitters of precepts, playing the same roles as the monks. Jesus also taught women freely. The first person Jesus revealed Himself to after His resurrection was a woman. Are we allowing women to be ordained priests and teachers?

The Buddha and his monks and nuns practiced voluntary poverty. They owned only three robes, one bowl, and one water filter. Are we able to live simply, content with just what we need? Or are our religious institutions simply building and acquiring more and more? The Buddha and his monks and nuns went begging every day to practice humility and to remain in contact with people in their society. Jesus in His time did very much the same. He did not own anything. He always made Himself available to people. He reached out and touched others in order to understand, to help, and to heal. The people He touched were mostly those who were suffering. Are the Sangha and the church of today in real touch with people? Are the churches today touching the poor and oppressed, or do they prefer to touch only the wealthy and powerful?

The Buddha always resisted violence and immorality. He withdrew his support from King Ajattasatru when the latter assassinated his father in order to ascend the throne. He tried to stop King Ajattasatru's efforts to start a war with the neighboring country of Vajji. Are our Sanghas doing the same— opposing social injustice and violence—or are we blessing wars and sending priests along with our armies to support the efforts of war? With utmost courage, Jesus taught a gospel of nonviolence. Is the church today practicing the same by its presence and behavior? Do the churches practice nonviolence and social justice, or do they align themselves with governments that practice violence and hatred? During the Vietnam War, the city of Ben Tre was destroyed in the name of salvation. The commander of the operation said, "We had to destroy Ben Tre in order to save it." Is it possible that a servant of the church blessed the troops being sent to such a war?

∽

JESUS NEEDS CHRISTIANS

For the Buddha to be present in the Sangha, we must practice in a way that keeps his teachings alive, and not confined to sermons and scriptures. The best way a Buddhist can keep the teachings of the Buddha alive is to live mindfully in the way the Buddha and his community lived. For Christians, the way to make the Holy Spirit truly present in the church is to practice thoroughly what Jesus lived and taught. It is not only true that Christians need Jesus, but Jesus needs Christians also for His energy to continue in this world.

SIX

A PEACEFUL HEART

COLLECTIVE AWARENESS

In the Sermon on the Mount, Jesus said, "Blessed are the peacemakers: for they shall be called the children of God." To work for peace, you must have a peaceful heart. When you do, you are the child of God. But many who work for peace are not at peace. They still have anger and frustration, and their work is not really peaceful. We cannot say that they are touching the Kingdom of God. To preserve peace, our hearts must be at peace with the world, with our brothers and our sisters. When we try to overcome evil with evil, we are not working for peace. If you say, "Saddam Hussein is evil. We have to prevent him from continuing to be evil," and if you then use the same means he has been using, you are exactly like him. Trying to overcome evil with evil is not the way to make peace.

Jesus also said, "Thou shalt not kill; and whosoever shall kill shall be in danger of the judgment. But I say unto you, that whosoever is angry with his brother without a cause shall be in danger of the judgment . . . whosoever shall say, 'Thou fool,' shall be in danger of hell fire." Jesus did not say that if you are angry with your brother, you will be put in a place called hell. He said that if you are angry with your brother, you are already in hell. Anger is hell. He also said that you don't need to kill with your body to be put in jail. You only need to kill in your mind and you are already there.

The death penalty is a sign of weakness, an expression of our fear and inability to know what to do to help the situation. Killing a person does not help him or us. We have to look collectively to find ways we can really help. Our enemy is not the other person, no matter what he or she has done. If we look deeply into ourselves, we can see that their act was a manifestation of our collective consciousness. We are all filled with violence, hatred, and fear, so why blame someone whose upbringing was without love or understanding? Educators, legislators, parents, journalists, filmmakers, economists, artists, poor people, rich people, all of us have to discuss the situation and see what we can do. Meditation can help. Meditation is not a drug to make us oblivious to our real problems. It should produce awareness in us and also in our society. For us to achieve results, our enlightenment has to be collective. How else can we end the cycle of violence? We ourselves have to contribute, in small and large ways, toward ending our own violence. Looking deeply at our own mind and our own life, we will begin to see what to do and what not to do to bring about a real change.

∞

LOOKING DEEPLY

We often think of peace as the absence of war, that if the powerful countries would reduce their weapons arsenals, we could have peace. But if we look deeply into the weapons, we see our own minds—our prejudices, fears, and ignorance. Even if we transport all the bombs to the moon, the roots of war and the roots of the bombs are still here, in our hearts and minds, and sooner or later we will make new bombs. To work for peace is to uproot war from ourselves and from the hearts of men and women. To prepare for war, to give millions of men and women the opportunity to practice killing day and night in their hearts, is to plant millions of seeds of violence, anger, frustration, and fear that will be passed on for generations to come.

"Ye have heard that it hath been said, An eye for an eye, and a tooth for a tooth. But I say unto you, That ye resist not evil: but whosoever shall smite thee on thy right cheek, turn to him the other also. And if any man will sue thee at the law, and take away thy coat, let him have thy cloak also." This is Jesus' teaching about revenge. When someone asks you for something, give it to him. When he wants to borrow something from you, lend it to him. How many of us actually practice this? There must be ways to solve our conflicts without killing. We must look at this. We have to find ways to help people get out of difficult situations, situations of conflict, without having to kill. Our collective wisdom and experience can be the torch lighting our path, showing us what to do. *Looking deeply together is the main task of a community or a church.*

∞

THE HIGHEST FORM
OF PRAYER

"Ye have heard that it hath been said, Thou shalt love thy neighbor, and hate thine enemy. But I say unto you, Love your enemies, bless them that curse you, do good to them that hate you, and pray for them which despitefully use you, and persecute you; that ye may be the children of your Father who is in heaven: for he maketh his sun to rise on the evil and on the good, and sendeth rain on the just and on the unjust." Many people pray to God because they want God to fulfill some of their needs. If they want to have a picnic, they ask God for a clear, sunny day. At the same time, farmers might pray for rain. If the weather is clear, the picnickers will say, "God is on our side; he answered our prayers." But if it rains, the farmers will say that God heard their prayers. This is the way we usually pray.

When you pray only for your own picnic and not for the farmers who need the rain, you are doing the opposite of what Jesus taught. Jesus said, "Love your enemies, bless them that curse you . . ." When you look deeply into your anger, you will see that the person you call your enemy is also suffering. As soon as you see that, the capacity of accepting and having compassion for him is there. Jesus called this "loving your enemy." When you are able to love your enemy, he or she is no longer your enemy. The idea of "enemy" vanishes and is replaced by the notion of someone who is suffering and needs your compassion. Doing this is sometimes easier than you might have imagined, but you need to practice. If you read the Bible but don't practice, it will not help much. In Buddhism, practicing the teaching of the Buddha is the highest form of prayer. The Buddha said, "If someone is standing on one shore and wants to go to the other shore, he has to either use a boat or swim across. He cannot just pray, 'Oh, other shore, please come over here for me to step across!' " To a Buddhist, praying without practicing is not real prayer.

∾

UNDERSTANDING BRINGS
LIBERATION

In Latin America, liberation theologians speak of God's preference, or "option," for the poor, the oppressed, and the marginalized. But I do not think God wants us to take sides, even with the poor. The rich also suffer, in many cases more than the poor! They may be rich materially, but many are poor spiritually, and they suffer a lot. I have known rich and famous people who have ended up committing suicide. I am certain that those with the highest understanding will be able to see the suffering in both the poor and the rich.

God embraces both rich and poor, and He wants them to understand each other, to share with each other their suffering and their happiness, and to work together for peace and social justice. We do not need to take sides. When we take sides, we misunderstand the will of God. I know it will be possible for some people to use these words to prolong social injustice, but that is an abuse of what I am saying. We have to find the *real causes* for social injustice, and when we do, we will not condemn a certain type of people. We will ask, Why has the situation of these people remained like that? All of us have the power of love and understanding. They are our best weapons. Any dualistic response, any response motivated by anger, will only make the situation worse.

When we practice looking deeply, we have the insight into what to do and what not to do for the situation to change. Everything depends on our way of looking. The existence of suffering is the First Noble Truth taught by the Buddha, and the causes of suffering are the second. When we look deeply at the First Truth, we discover the second. After seeing the Second Truth, we see the next truth, which is the way of liberation. Everything depends on our understanding of the whole situation. Once we understand, our life style will change accordingly and our actions will never help the oppressors strengthen their stand. Looking deeply does not mean being inactive. We become very active with our understanding. *Nonviolence does not mean non-action. Nonviolence means we act with love and compassion.*

∽

UNDERSTANDING BRINGS COMPASSION

Before the Vietnamese monk Thich Quang Duc burned himself alive in 1963, he meditated for several weeks and then wrote very loving letters to his government, his church, and his fellow monks and nuns explaining why he had reached that decision. When you are motivated by love and the willingness to help others attain understanding, even self-immolation can be a compassionate act. When Jesus allowed Himself to be crucified, He was acting in the same way, motivated by the desire to wake people up, to restore understanding and compassion, and to save people. When you are motivated by anger or discrimination, even if you act in exactly the same way, you are doing the opposite.

When you read Thich Quang Duc's letters, you know very clearly that he was not motivated by the wish to oppose or destroy but by the desire to communicate. When you are caught in a war in which the great powers have huge weapons and complete control of the mass media, you have to do something extraordinary to make yourself heard. Without access to radio, television, or the press, you have to create new ways to help the world understand the situation you are in. Self-immolation can be such a means. If you do it out of love, you act very much as Jesus did on the cross and as Gandhi did in India. Gandhi fasted, not with anger, but with compassion, not only toward his countrymen but also toward the British. These great men all knew that it is the truth that sets us free, and they did everything they could to make the truth known.

Buddhist and Christian practice is the same—to make the truth available—the truth about ourselves, the truth about our brothers and sisters, the truth about our situation. This is the work of writers, preachers, the media, and also practitioners. Each day, we practice looking deeply into ourselves and into the situation of our brothers and sisters. It is the most serious work we can do.

❦

UNDERSTANDING TRANSFORMS

If while we practice we are not aware that the world is suffering, that children are dying of hunger, that social injustice is going on everywhere, we are not practicing mindfulness. We are just trying to escape. But anger is not enough. Jesus told us to love our enemy. "Father, forgive them, for they know not what they do." This teaching helps us know how to look at the person we consider to be the cause of our suffering. If we practice looking deeply into his situation and the causes of how he came to be the way he is now, and if we visualize ourselves as being born in his condition, we may see that we could have become exactly like him. When we do that, compassion arises in us naturally, and we see that the other person is to be helped and not punished. In that moment, our anger *transforms itself* into the energy of compassion. Suddenly, the one we have been calling our enemy becomes our brother or sister. This is the true teaching of Jesus. Looking deeply is one of the most effective ways to transform our anger, prejudices, and discrimination. We practice as an individual, and we also practice as a group.

❧

UNDERSTANDING
OURSELVES HELPS US
UNDERSTAND OTHERS

In Buddhism, we speak of salvation by understanding. We see that it is the lack of understanding
that creates suffering. Understanding is the power
that can liberate us. It is the key that can unlock the
door to the prison of suffering. If we do not practice
understanding, we do not avail ourselves of the most
powerful instrument that can free us and other living
beings from suffering. True love is possible only
with real understanding. Buddhist meditation—
stopping, calming, and looking deeply—is to help us
understand better. In each of us is a seed of understanding. That seed is God. It is also the Buddha. If
you doubt the existence of that seed of understanding, you doubt God and you doubt the Buddha.

When Gandhi said that love is the force that can
liberate, he meant we have to love our enemy. Even
if our enemy is cruel, even if he is crushing us, sow-
ing terror and injustice, we have to love him. This is
the message of Jesus. But how can we love our enemy? There is only one way—to understand him.
We have to understand why he is that way, how he
has come to be like that, why he does not see things

the way we do. Understanding a person brings us the power to love and accept him. And the moment we love and accept him, he ceases to be our enemy. To "love our enemy" is impossible, because the moment we love him, he is no longer our enemy.

To love him, we must practice deep looking in order to understand him. If we do, we accept him, we love him, and we also accept and love ourselves. As Buddhists or Christians, we cannot question that understanding is the most important component for transformation. If we talk to each other, if we organize a dialogue, it is because we believe there is a possibility that we can understand the other person better. When we understand another person, we understand ourselves better. And when we understand ourselves better, we understand the other person better, too.

～

UNDERSTANDING BRINGS FORGIVENESS

"Forgive us our trespasses, as we forgive those who trespass against us." Everyone makes mistakes. If we are mindful, we see that some of our actions in the past have caused others to suffer, and some actions of others have made us suffer. We want to be forgiving. We want to begin anew. "You, my brother or sister, have wronged me in the past. I now understand that it was because you were suffering and did not see clearly. I no longer feel anger toward you." You cannot force yourself to forgive. Only when you understand what has happened can you have compassion for the other person and forgive him or her. That kind of forgiveness is the fruit of awareness. When you are mindful, you can see the many causes that led the other person to make you suffer, and when you see this, forgiveness and release arise naturally. Putting the teachings of Jesus and the Buddha into practice is always helpful.

SEVEN

FOR A FUTURE

TO BE POSSIBLE

REROOTING

There is a deep malaise in society. We can send e-mail and faxes anywhere in the world, we have pagers and cellular telephones, and yet in our families and neighborhoods we do not speak to each other. There is a kind of vacuum inside us, and we attempt to fill it by eating, reading, talking, smoking, drinking, watching TV, going to movies, and even overworking. We absorb so much violence and insecurity every day that we are like time bombs ready to explode. We need to find a cure for our illness.

Many of our young people are uprooted. They no longer believe in the traditions of their parents and grandparents, and they have not found anything else to replace them. Spiritual leaders need to address this very real issue, but most simply do not know what to do. They have not been able to transmit the deepest values of their traditions, perhaps because they themselves have not fully understood or experienced them. When a priest does not embody the living values of a tradition, he or she cannot transmit them to the next generation. He can only wear the outer garments and pass along the superficial forms. When the living values are absent, rituals and dogmas are lifeless, rigid, and even oppressive. Combined with a lack of understanding of people's real needs and a general lack of tolerance, it is little wonder that the young feel alienated within these institutions.

Buddhism, like Christianity and other traditions, has to renew itself in order to respond to the needs of the people of our time. Many young people all over the world have abandoned their church because church leaders have not caught up with the changes in society. They cannot speak to the young people in the kind of language the young can understand.

They cannot transmit the jewels they have received from their ancestral teachers to the young. That is why so many young people are left with nothing to believe in. They feel uneasy with their church, their society, their culture, and their family. They don't see anything worthwhile, beautiful, or true.

We need roots to be able to stand straight and grow strong. When young people come to Plum Village, I always encourage them to practice in a way that will help them go back to their own tradition and get rerooted. If they succeed at becoming reintegrated, they will be an important instrument in transforming and renewing their tradition. After an interfaith retreat in Santa Barbara, one young man told me, "Thây, I feel more Jewish than ever. I will tell my rabbi that a Buddhist monk inspired me to go back to him." People from other traditions said the same thing.

THE JEWELS OF OUR OWN TRADITION

In East Asia, every home has a family altar. Whenever there is an important event in the family, such as the birth of a child, we offer incense and announce the news to our ancestors. If our son is about to go to college, we make an offering and announce that tomorrow our son will leave for college. When we return home after a long trip, the first thing we do is offer incense to our ancestors and announce that we are home. When we practice this way, we always feel deeply rooted in the family.

I encourage my students of Western origin to do the same. When we respect our blood ancestors and our spiritual ancestors, we feel rooted. If we can find ways to cherish and develop our spiritual heritage, we will avoid the kind of alienation that is destroying society, and we will become whole again. We must encourage others, especially young people, to go back to their traditions and rediscover the jewels that are there. Learning to touch deeply the jewels of our own tradition will allow us to understand and appreciate the values of other traditions, and this will benefit everyone.

≈

CULTIVATING COMPASSION

Precepts in Buddhism and commandments in Judaism and Christianity are important jewels that we need to study and practice. They provide guidelines that can help us transform our suffering. Looking deeply at these precepts and commandments, we can learn the art of living in beauty. The Five Wonderful Precepts of Buddhism—reverence for life, generosity, responsible sexual behavior, speaking and listening deeply, and ingesting only wholesome substances—can contribute greatly to the happiness of the family and society. I have recently rephrased them to address the problems of our times:

> 1.   *Aware of the suffering caused by the destruction of life, I vow to cultivate compassion and learn ways to protect the lives of people, animals, plants, and minerals. I am determined not to kill, not to let others kill, and not to condone any act of killing in the world, in my thinking and in my way of life.*

The First Precept is born from the awareness that lives everywhere are being destroyed. We see the suffering caused by the destruction of life, and we vow to cultivate compassion and use it as a source of energy for the protection of people, animals, plants, and minerals. No act of killing can be justified. And not to kill is not enough. We must also learn ways to prevent others from killing. We cannot condone any act of killing, even in our minds. According to the Buddha, the mind is the base of all actions. When you believe, for example, that yours is the only way for humankind, millions of people might be killed because of that idea. We have to look deeply every day to practice this precept well. Every time we buy or consume something, we may be condoning some form of killing.

To practice nonviolence, first of all we must learn to deal peacefully with ourselves. In us, there is a certain amount of violence and a certain amount of nonviolence. Depending on the state of our being, our response to things will be more or less nonviolent. With mindfulness—the practice of peace—we can begin by working to transform the wars in ourselves. Conscious breathing helps us do this. But no one can practice this precept perfectly. We should not be too proud about being a vegetarian, for example. We must acknowledge that the water in which we boil our vegetables contains many tiny microorganisms, not to mention the vegetables themselves. But even if we cannot be completely nonviolent, by being vegetarian we are going in the direction of nonviolence. If we want to head north, we can use the North Star to guide us, but it is impossible to arrive at the North Star. Our effort is only to proceed in that direction. If we create true harmony within ourselves, we will know how to deal with family, friends, and society.

Life is so precious, yet in our daily lives we are

usually carried away by our forgetfulness, anger, and worries. The practice of the First Precept is a celebration of reverence for life. When we appreciate and honor the beauty of life, we will make every effort to dwell deeply in the present moment and protect all life.

∞

CULTIVATING
LOVING-KINDNESS

2. Aware of the suffering caused by exploitation, social injustice, stealing, and oppression, I vow to cultivate loving-kindness and learn ways to work for the well-being of people, animals, plants, and minerals. I vow to practice generosity by sharing my time, energy, and material resources with those who are in real need. I am determined not to steal and not to possess anything that should belong to others. I will respect the property of others, but I will prevent others from profiting from human suffering or the suffering of other species on Earth.

The Five Precepts inter-are. When you practice one precept deeply, you practice all five. The First Precept is about taking life, which is a form of stealing. When we meditate on the Second Precept, we see that stealing, in the forms of exploitation, social injustice, and oppression, is an act of killing.

Instead of stealing, we practice generosity. In Buddhism, we say there are three kinds of gifts: (1) the gift of material resources, (2) the gift of helping people rely on themselves, and (3) the gift of nonfear. But it takes time to practice generosity. Sometimes one pill or a little rice could save the life of a child, but we do not think we have the time to help. The best use of our time is being generous and really being present with others. People of our time tend to overwork, even when they are not in great need of money. We seem to take refuge in our work in order to avoid confronting our real sorrow and inner turmoil. We express our love and care for others by working hard, but if we do not have time for the people we love, if we cannot make ourselves available to them, how can we say that we love them?

True love needs mindfulness. We have to take the time to acknowledge the presence of the person we love. "Darling, I know you are there, and I am happy." This cannot be done if we can't free ourselves from our preoccupations and our forgetfulness. In order to acknowledge the presence of our beloved one, we have to offer our own true presence. Without the practice of establishing ourselves in the here and in the now, this seems impossible. Mindful time spent with the person we love is the fullest expression of true love and real generosity. One twelve-year-old boy, when asked by his father what he would like for his birthday, said, "Daddy, I want you!" His father was rarely at home. He was quite wealthy, but he worked all the time to provide for his family. His son was a bell of mindfulness for him. The little boy understood that the greatest gift we can offer our loved ones is our true presence.

☙

THE ONENESS OF
BODY AND MIND

3.   Aware of the suffering caused by sexual misconduct, I vow to cultivate responsibility and learn ways to protect the safety and integrity of individuals, couples, families, and society. I am determined not to engage in sexual relations without love and a long-term commitment. To preserve the happiness of myself and others, I am determined to respect my commitments and the commitments of others. I will do everything in my power to protect children from sexual abuse

*and to prevent couples and families from being
broken by sexual misconduct.*

So many individuals, children, couples, and families
have been destroyed by sexual misconduct. To practice the Third Precept is to heal ourselves and heal
our society. This is mindful living.

The feeling of loneliness is universal. We believe
in a naive way that having a sexual relationship will
make us feel less lonely. But without communication on the level of the heart and spirit, a sexual
relationship will only widen the gap and harm us
both. We know that violating this precept causes
severe problems, but still we do not practice it seri-
ously. Couples engage in infidelity; and jealousy,
anger, and despair are the result. When the children
grow up, they repeat the same mistakes, yet the violation of this precept continues to be encouraged in
magazines, TV shows, films, books, and so on. We
constantly encounter themes that arouse sexual desire, often coupled with themes of violence. If our
collective consciousness is filled with violent sexual
seeds, why should we be surprised when there is
sexual abuse of children, rape, and other violent
acts?

In the Buddhist tradition, we speak of the oneness of body and mind. Whatever happens to the

body also happens to the mind. The sanity of the body is the sanity of the mind; the violation of the body is the violation of the mind. A sexual relationship is an act of communion between body and spirit. This is a very important encounter, not to be done in a casual manner. In our soul there are certain areas—memories, pain, secrets—that are private, that we would share only with the person we love and trust the most. We do not open our heart and show it to just anyone.

The same is true of our body. Our bodies have areas that we do not want anyone to touch or approach unless he or she is the one we respect, trust, and love the most. When we are approached casually or carelessly, with an attitude that is less than tender, we feel insulted in our body and soul. Someone who approaches us with respect, tenderness, and utmost care is offering us deep communication, deep communion. It is only in that case that we will not feel hurt, misused, or abused, even a little. This cannot be attained unless there is true love and commitment. Casual sex cannot be described as love. Love is deep, beautiful, and whole, integrating body and spirit.

True love contains respect. In my tradition, husband and wife are expected to respect each other like guests, and when you practice this kind of respect, your love and happiness will continue for a long time. In sexual relationships, respect is one of the most important elements. Sexual communion should be like a rite, a ritual performed in mindfulness with great respect, care, and love. Mere desire is not love. Without the communion of souls, the coming together of the two bodies can create division, widening the gap and causing much suffering.

Love is much more responsible. It has care in it and it involves the willingness and capacity to understand and to make the other person happy. In true love, happiness is not an individual matter. If the other person is not happy, it will be impossible for us to be happy ourselves. True happiness is not possible without a certain degree of calmness and peace in our heart and in our body. Passion or excitement contains within it the element of disturbance. True love is a process of learning and practice that brings in more elements of peace, harmony, and happiness.

The phrase "long-term commitment" does not express the depth of love we feel for our partner, but we have to say something so people understand. A long-term commitment is only a beginning. We also need the support of friends and other people. That is why we have a wedding ceremony. Two families join together with other friends to witness the fact that the couple has come together to live. The priest and the marriage license are just symbols. What is important is that the commitment is witnessed by friends and both of the families. "Responsibility" is the key word. The Third Precept should be practiced by everyone.

∽

MORE THAN
ONE ROOT

If a Buddhist woman wants to marry a Christian man (or vice versa), should we encourage them? The woman will have to learn and practice her husband's tradition, and the man will have to learn and practice his wife's tradition. Then, instead of having just one spiritual root, they will have two. But can a person have two spiritual roots at the same time? Can both of them learn Christianity and Buddhism and practice both traditions? We know that when someone does not have any root, he or she will suffer tremendously. But what about the question of having more than one root?

Before I met Christianity, my only spiritual ancestor was the Buddha. But when I met beautiful men and women who are Christians, I came to know Jesus as a great teacher. Since that day, Jesus

Christ has become one of my spiritual ancestors. As I have mentioned, on the altar of my hermitage in France, I have statues of Buddhas and bodhisattvas and also an image of Jesus Christ. I do not feel any conflict within me. Instead I feel stronger because I have more than one root.

Can we allow young people of different traditions to marry each other freely, with our benediction? Can we encourage them to practice both traditions and enrich each other?

∾

UNMINDFUL SPEECH CAN KILL

4. Aware of the suffering caused by unmindful speech and the inability to listen to others, I vow to cultivate loving speech and deep listening in order to bring joy and happiness to others and relieve others of their suffering. Knowing that words can create happiness or suffering, I vow to learn to speak truthfully, with words that inspire self-confidence, joy, and hope. I am determined not to spread news that I do not know to be certain and not to criticize or condemn things of which I am not sure. I will refrain from uttering words that can cause division

or discord, or that can cause the family or the
community to break. I will make all efforts to
reconcile and resolve all conflicts, however small.

In the Buddhist tradition, the Fourth Precept is described as refraining from these four actions: (1) Not telling the truth. If it's black, you say it's white. (2) Exaggerating. You make something up, or describe something as more beautiful than it actually is, or as ugly when it is not so ugly. (3) Forked tongue. You go to one person and say one thing and then you go to another person and say the opposite. (4) Filthy language. You insult or abuse people.

This precept admonishes us not to lie, not to say things that destroy friendships and relationships, but to use wholesome, loving speech. It is as important as the Third Precept in preventing families from being broken. Speaking unmindfully or irresponsibly can destroy us, because when we lie, we lose faith in our own beauty and we lose the trust of others. We have to dissolve all prejudices, barriers, and walls and empty ourselves in order to listen and look deeply before we utter even one word. When we are mindful of our words, it helps us, our families, and our society. We also need to practice the Fourth Precept as individuals and as a nation. We have to work to undo the misunderstandings that exist between the

United States and Vietnam, France and Germany, Norway and Sweden, and so on. And we must not underestimate the misunderstandings between religious traditions. Church leaders, diplomats, and all of us need to practice this precept carefully.

Never in the history of humankind have we had so many means of communication, yet we remain islands. There is little real communication between the members of one family, between the individuals in society, and between nations. We have not cultivated the arts of listening and speaking. We have to learn ways to communicate again. When we cannot communicate, we get sick, and as our sickness worsens, our suffering spills onto other people. When it has become too difficult to share and to communicate with those in our family, we want to go to a psychotherapist, hoping that he or she will listen to our suffering. Psychotherapists are also human beings. There are those who can listen deeply to us and those who, because they themselves have suffered so much, do not have the capacity. Psychotherapists have to train themselves in the art of listening with calm and compassion. How can someone who has so much suffering within himself or herself, so much anger, irritation, fear, and despair, listen deeply to us? If you wish to see a psychotherapist, try to find someone who is happy and who can communicate well with his or her spouse, children, friends, and society.

Training ourselves in the art of mindful breathing is crucial for knowing how to take care of our emotions. First, we recognize the presence of, for example, anger in us, and we allow it to be. We do not try to suppress it or express it. We just bring the energy of mindfulness to our anger and allow our mindfulness to take care of it the way a mother holds her baby when it begins to cry. We do this by practicing mindful breathing, while sitting or while walking. Walking alone in a park or along a river, coordinating our steps with our breath, is a very effective way to care for our anger, to calm it down.

In his Discourse on Mindful Breathing, the Buddha taught, "Breathing in, I recognize my feeling. Breathing out, I calm my feeling." If you practice this, not only will your feeling be calmed down but the energy of mindfulness will also help you see into the nature and roots of your anger. Mindfulness helps you be concentrated and look deeply. This is true meditation. The insight will come after some time of practice. You will see the truth about yourself and the truth about the person who you thought to be the cause of your suffering. This insight will release you from your anger and transform the roots of anger in you. The transformation in you will also help transform the other person.

Mindful speaking can bring real happiness, and unmindful speech can kill. When someone tells us something that makes us happy, that is a wonderful gift. But sometimes someone says something to us that is so cruel and distressing that we feel like committing suicide. We lose our *joie de vivre*.

The Fourth Precept is also linked to the Second Precept, on stealing. Many people have to lie in order to succeed as politicians or salespersons. A corporate director of communications told me that if he were allowed to tell the truth about his company's products, people would not buy them. He says positive things about the products that he knows are not true, and he refrains from speaking about their negative effects. He knows he is lying, and he feels terrible about it. Many people are caught in this kind of situation. In politics, people lie to get votes.

This precept is also linked with the Third Precept, on sexual responsibility. When someone says, "I love you," it may be a lie. It may just be an expression of desire. So much advertising is linked with sex. There is a saying in Vietnamese: "It doesn't cost anything to have loving speech." We only need to choose our words carefully, and we can make other people happy. To use words mindfully, with loving-kindness, is to practice generosity. Therefore this precept is linked directly to the Second Precept. We can make many people happy just by practicing loving speech. Again, we see the interbeing nature of the Five Precepts.

∽

MINDFUL CONSUMING

5.   *Aware of the suffering caused by unmindful consumption, I vow to cultivate good health, both physical and mental, for myself, my family, and my society by practicing mindful eating, drinking, and consuming. I vow to ingest only items that preserve peace, well-being, and joy in my body, in my consciousness, and in the collective body and consciousness of my family and society. I am determined not to use alcohol or any other intoxicant or to ingest foods or other items that contain toxins, such as certain TV programs, magazines, books, films, and conversations. I am aware that to damage my body or my consciousness with these poisons is to betray my ancestors, my parents, my society, and future generations. I will work to transform violence, fear, anger, and confusion in myself and*

in society by practicing a diet for myself and for
society. I understand that a proper diet is crucial
for self-transformation and for the transformation
of society.

In modern life, people think that their body belongs to them and they can do anything they want to it. When they make such a determination, the law supports them. This is one of the manifestations of individualism. But, according to the teachings of emptiness, non-self, and interbeing, your body is not yours alone. It also belongs to your ancestors, your parents, future generations, and all other living beings. Everything, even the trees and the clouds, has come together to bring about the presence of your body. Keeping your body healthy is the best way to express your gratitude to the whole cosmos, to all ancestors, and also not to betray future generations. You practice this precept for everyone. If you are healthy, everyone can benefit from it. When you are able to get out of the shell of your small self, you will see that you are interrelated to everyone and everything, that your every act is linked with the whole of humankind and the whole cosmos. To keep yourself healthy in body and mind is to be kind to all beings. The Fifth Precept is about health and healing.

This precept tells us not to ingest poisons that

can destroy our minds and bodies. We should especially avoid alcohol and other intoxicants that cause so much suffering to the individuals involved and to the victims of intoxication—abused family members, those injured in automobile accidents, and so on. Alcohol abuse is one of the main symptoms of the malaise of our times. We know that those who are addicted to alcohol need to abstain one hundred percent. But the Buddha also asked those who have only one glass of wine a week also to refrain from drinking. Why? Because we practice for everyone, including those who have a propensity toward alcoholism. If we give up our glass of wine, it is to show our children, our friends, and our society that our life is not for ourselves alone, but for our ancestors, future generations, and our society also. To stop drinking one glass of wine a week, even if it has not brought us any harm, is a deep practice, the insight of someone who knows that everything we do is for our ancestors and all future generations. I think that the use of drugs by so many young people could be stopped with this kind of insight.

When someone offers you a glass of wine, you can smile and decline, saying, "No, thank you. I do not drink alcohol. I would be grateful if you would bring me a glass of juice or water." If you do it gently, with a smile, your refusal is very helpful. It sets an example for many friends, including the children who are present. There are so many delicious and healthy beverages available—why must we continue to honor a beverage that brings about so much suffering? I have asked rabbis, priests, and nuns if they think it would be possible to substitute grape juice for wine in Sabbath rituals, the Eucharist, and other sacramental occasions, and they have said yes.

We must also be careful to avoid ingesting toxins in the form of violent TV programs, video games, movies, magazines, and books. When we watch that kind of violence, we water our own negative seeds, or tendencies, and eventually we will think and act out of those seeds. Because of the violent toxins in so many people's minds, and in our minds, too, it has become dangerous to walk alone at night in many cities. Young people stare at television sets hour after hour, and their minds are invaded by programs selected by irresponsible producers.

The Fifth Precept urges us to find wholesome, spiritual nourishment not only for ourselves but also for our children and future generations. Wholesome, spiritual nourishment can be found by looking at the blue sky, the spring blossoms, or the eyes of a child. The most basic meditation practice of becoming aware of our bodies, our minds, and our world can lead us into a far more rich and fulfilling state than drugs ever could. We can celebrate the joys that are available in these simple pleasures.

The use of alcohol and drugs is causing so much damage to our societies and families. Governments use airplanes, guns, and armies to try to stop the flow of drugs, with little success. Drug users know how destructive their habit is, but they cannot stop. There is so much pain and loneliness inside them, and the use of alcohol and drugs helps them to forget for a while. Once people are addicted to alcohol or drugs, they might do anything to get the drugs they need—lie, steal, rob, or even kill. Trying to stop the drug traffic is not the best use of our resources. Offering education, wholesome alternatives, and hope, and encouraging people to practice the Fifth Precept are much better solutions. To restore our balance and transform the pain and loneliness that are already in us, we have to study and practice the art of touching and ingesting the refreshing, nourishing, and healing elements that are already available. We have to practice together as a family, a community, and a nation. The practice of mindful consuming should become part of our national health policy. Making it so should be a top priority.

The Five Wonderful Precepts are the right medicine to heal us. We need only to observe ourselves and those around us to see the truth. Our stability and the stability of our families and society cannot be obtained without the practice of these precepts. If you look at individuals and families who are unstable and unhappy, you will be astonished to see how many of them do not practice these healthy and life-affirming precepts. You can make the diagnosis yourself and then know that the medicine is available. Practicing these precepts is the best way to restore stability in our families and our society.

The practice of mindfulness is to be aware of what is going on. Once we are able to see deeply the suffering and the roots of the suffering, we will be motivated to act, to practice. The energy we need is not fear or anger, but understanding and compassion. There is no need to blame or condemn. Those who destroy themselves, their families, and their society are not doing it intentionally. Their pain and loneliness are overwhelming, and they want to escape. They need to be helped, not punished. Only understanding and compassion on a collective level can liberate us. The practice of the Five Wonderful Precepts is the practice of mindfulness and compassion. I urge you to practice them as they are presented here, or go back to your own tradition and shed light on the jewels that are already there.

≋

REAL LOVE NEVER ENDS

In Judaism, we are encouraged to enjoy the world as long as we are aware that it is God Himself. But there are limits, and the Ten Commandments, which God gave Moses on Mount Sinai, express this. The Ten Commandments are a precious jewel of the Judeo-Christian heritage, helping us know what to do and what not to do in order to cherish God throughout our daily life.

All precepts and commandments are about love and understanding. Jesus gave His disciples the commandment to love God with all their being and to love their neighbors as themselves. In First Corinthians, it says, "Love is patient. Love is kind. Love is not envious, arrogant, or rude. It does not rejoice in wrong. It does not insist on its own way. It is not irritable or resentful. It does not rejoice in wrongdoing, but rejoices in the truth." This is very close to the teachings of love and compassion in Buddhism.

"Love bears all things, believes all things, endures all things." Love has no limits. Love never ends. Love is reborn and reborn and reborn. The love and care of the Christ is reborn in each of us, as is the love of the Buddha. If we invoke the name of Buddha or pray to Christ but do not practice love and understanding ourselves, something is wrong. If we love someone, we have to be patient. We can only help a person transform his or her negative seeds if we are patient and kind.

To take good care of yourself and to take good care of living beings and of the environment is the best way to love God. This love is possible when there is the understanding that you are not separate from other beings or the environment. This understanding cannot be merely intellectual. It must be experiential, the insight gained by deep touching and deep looking in a daily life of prayer, contemplation, and meditation.

"Love does not rejoice in wrongdoing." Love instructs us not to act in ways that will cause suffering now or in the future. We can discern when something that seems to be joyful has the capacity to destroy future happiness, so we do not abuse alcohol, ingest unhealthy foods, or hurt others by our words. Real love never ends. It will be reborn and reborn.

❧

PRACTICING AND SHARING

Peace activist A. J. Muste said, "There is no way to peace, peace is the way." He meant that we can realize peace right in the present moment with each look, smile, word, and action. Peace is not just an end. Each step we make should be peace, should be joy, should be happiness. Precepts and commandments help us dwell in peace, knowing what to do and what not to do in the present moment. They are treasures that lead us along a path of beauty, wholesomeness, and truth. They contain the wisdom of our spiritual traditions, and when we practice them, our lives become a true expression of our faith, and our well-being becomes an encouragement to our friends and to society.

Our happiness and the happiness of others depends on not only a few people becoming mindful and responsible. The whole nation has to be aware. Precepts and commandments must be respected and practiced by individuals and by the entire nation. When so many families are broken, the fabric of society is torn. We must look deeply at this in order to understand the nature of these precepts and commandments. Everyone must join in the work. For our world to have a future, we need basic behavioral guidelines. They are the best medicine available to protect us from the violence that is everywhere. Practicing precepts or commandments is not a matter of suppression or limiting our freedom. Precepts and commandments offer us a wonderful way to live, and we can practice them with joy. It is not a matter of forcing ourselves or others to obey rules.

No single tradition monopolizes the truth. We must glean the best values of all traditions and work together to remove the tensions between traditions in order to give peace a chance. We need to join together and look deeply for ways to help people get rerooted. We need to propose the best physical, mental, and spiritual health plan for our nation and for the earth. For a future to be possible, I urge you to study and practice the best values of your religious tradition and to share them with young people in ways they can understand. If we meditate together as a family, a community, a city, and a nation, we will be able to identify the causes of our suffering and find ways out.

EIGHT

TAKING REFUGE

A SAFE ISLAND

In every religious tradition there is devotional practice and transformational practice. Devotion means relying more on yourself and the path you are following. Both of these are paths that can help us relieve suffering. But being devoted to the Dharma can be different from practicing the Dharma. When you say, "I take refuge in the Dharma," you are showing your faith in it, but that may not be the

same as practicing. When you say, "I want to become a doctor," you express your determination to
practice medicine. But to become a doctor, you
have to spend seven or eight years studying and
practicing medicine. When you say, "I take refuge
in the Buddha, the Dharma, and the Sangha," this
may be only the willingness to practice. It is not
because you make a statement that you are already
practicing. You enter the path of transformation
when you begin to practice the things you pronounce.

But pronouncing words does have an effect.
When you say, "I am determined to study medicine," that already has an impact on your life, even
before you apply to medical school. You want to do
it, and because of your willingness and desire, you
will find a way to go to school. When you say, "I
take refuge in the Dharma," you are expressing confidence in the Dharma. You see the Dharma as
something positive, and you want to orient yourself
toward it. That is devotion. When you apply the
Dharma in your daily life, that is transformational
practice.

Mindfulness is the key. When you become aware
of something, you begin to have enlightenment.
When you drink a glass of water and are aware that

you are drinking a glass of water deeply with your whole being, enlightenment is there in its initial form. To be enlightened is always to be enlightened about something. I am enlightened about the fact that I am drinking a glass of water. I can obtain joy, peace, and happiness just because of that enlightenment. When you look at the blue sky and are aware of it, the sky becomes real, and you become real. That is enlightenment, and enlightenment brings about true life and true happiness. The substance of a Buddha is mindfulness. Every time you practice conscious breathing, you are a living Buddha. To go back to yourself and dwell in mindfulness is the best practice in difficult moments. Mindfulness of breathing is your island, where you can be safe and happy, knowing that whatever happens, you are doing your best thing. This is the way to take refuge in the Buddha, not as mere devotion but as a transformational practice. You do not have to abandon this world. You do not have to go to Heaven or wait for the future to have refuge. You can take refuge here and now. You only need to dwell deeply in the present moment.

∞

MINDFULNESS IS
THE REFUGE

In Buddhism, we take refuge in Three Jewels—
Buddha, Dharma, and Sangha. These refuges are a
very deep practice. They are the Buddhist trinity:

I take refuge in the Buddha,
the one who shows me the way in this life.
I take refuge in the Dharma,
the way of understanding and love.
I take refuge in the Sangha,
the community that lives in harmony and awareness.

Many years ago I encountered some children on
a beach in Sri Lanka. It had been a long time since I
had seen children like that, barefoot children on a
very green island with no sign of industrial pollu-
tion. These were not children of slums; they were of
the countryside. I saw them, and to me they formed
a beautiful part of nature. As I stood on the beach
alone, the children just ran toward me. We didn't
know each other's language, so I put my arms
around their shoulders—all six of them, and we
stood like that for a long time. Suddenly I realized
that if I chanted a prayer in the ancient Buddhist

language of Pali, they might recognize it, so I began to chant, *"Buddham saranam gacchami"* (I take refuge in the Buddha). They not only recognized it, they continued the chant. Four of them joined their palms and chanted, while the other two stood respectfully. This chant is a common prayer, like the Our Father. "I take refuge in the Buddha. I take refuge in the Dharma. I take refuge in the Sangha."

I motioned to the two children who were not chanting to join us. They smiled, placed their palms together and chanted in Pali, "'I take refuge in Mother Mary." The music of their prayer did not differ much from the Buddhist one. Then I embraced each child. They were a little surprised, but I felt very much at one with each of them. They had given me a feeling of deep serenity and peace. We all need a place that is safe and wholesome enough for us to return for refuge. In Buddhism, that refuge is mindfulness.

∾

THE FOUNDATION OF
STABILITY AND CALM

When we were in our mother's womb, we felt secure—protected from heat, cold, and hunger. But the moment we were born and came into contact with the world's suffering, we began to cry. Since then, we have yearned to return to the security of our mother's womb. We long for permanence, but everything is changing. We desire an absolute, but even what we call our "self" is impermanent. We seek a place where we can feel safe and secure, a place we can rely on for a long time. When we touch the ground, we feel the stability of the earth and feel confident. When we observe the steadiness of the sunshine, the air, and the trees, we know that we can count on the sun to rise each day and the air and the trees to be there tomorrow. When we build a house, we build it on ground that is solid. Before putting our trust in others, we need to choose friends who are stable, on whom we can rely. "Taking refuge" is not based on blind faith or wishful thinking. It is gauged by our real experience.

We all need something good, beautiful, and true to believe in. To take refuge in mindfulness, our capacity of being aware of what is going on in the present moment, is safe and not at all abstract. When we drink a glass of water and know we are drinking a glass of water, that is mindfulness. When we sit, walk, stand, or breathe and know that we are sitting, walking, standing, or breathing, we touch the seed of mindfulness in us, and, after a few days, our mindfulness will grow stronger. Mindfulness is the light that shows us the way. It is the living Buddha inside of us. Mindfulness gives rise to insight, awakening, and love. We all have the seed of mindfulness within us and, through the practice of conscious breathing, we can learn to touch it. When we take refuge in the Buddhist trinity—Buddha, Dharma, and Sangha—it means to take refuge in our mindfulness, our mindful breathing, and the five elements that comprise our self.

> *Breathing in, breathing out,*
> *Buddha is my mindfulness, shining near, shining*
>   *far.*
> *Dharma is my conscious breathing, calming my body*
>   *and mind.*
> *I am free.*
> *Breathing in, breathing out,*
> *Sangha is my five skandhas, working in harmony.*
> *Taking refuge in myself,*
> *Going back to myself.*
> *I am free.*

When we practice this exercise, it takes us directly to a place of peace and stability, to the most calm and stable place we can go. The Buddha taught, "Be an island unto yourself. Take refuge in yourself and not in anything else." This island is right mindfulness, the awakened nature, the foundation of stability and calm that resides in each of us. This island shines light on our path and helps us see what to do and what not to do. When our five *skandhas*—form, feelings, perceptions, mental states, and consciousness—are in harmony, there will naturally be right action and peace. Conscious breathing brings about calmness and harmony. Aware that practicing this way is the best thing we can do, we will feel solid within and we will be a true vehicle for helping others.

∽

EMBRACING,
NOT FIGHTING

In the Orthodox Christian church, the idea of the Trinity is quite profound. Sometimes our Orthodox friends call the Trinity their "social program." They begin with the Holy Spirit and the Son. The Father belongs to the realm of inexpressibility, but it is possible to touch the Son and the Holy Spirit. We have the capacity to recognize the presence of the Holy Spirit whenever and wherever it manifests. It, too, is the presence of mindfulness, understanding, and love, the energy that animates

Jesus and helps us recognize the living Christ. When a Christian makes the Sign of the Cross or says the names of the Father, the Son, and the Holy Spirit, she is taking refuge.

The Buddha said that his body of teachings would remain with his students but that it was up to them to make it last. If we don't practice, there will be only books and tapes, but if we practice, the Dharma body will be a living Dharma. Dharmakaya later came to mean soul of the Buddha, spirit of the Buddha, true Buddha, or nature of the Buddha. It developed an ontological flavor—ground of all being, ground of all enlightenment. Finally, it became equivalent to suchness, nirvana, and *tathagatagarbha* (the womb of the Tathagata). That is a natural development. The Dharma is the door that opens to many meanings.

In the Greek Orthodox church, the idea of deification, that a person is a microcosm of God, is very inspiring. It is close to the Asian tradition that states that the body of a human being is a minicosmos. God made humans so that humans can become God. A human being is a mini-God, a *micro-theos* who has been created in order to participate in the divinity of God. Deification is made not only of the spirit but of the body of a human also. According to the teaching of the Trinity in the Orthodox church, the Father is the source of divinity who engenders the Son. With the Word *(Logos)*, He brings about the Spirit that is alive in the Son. This is very much like the nondual nature of Buddha, Dharma, and Sangha.

Alphonse Daudet wrote about a shepherd on a mountain who made the Sign of the Cross when he saw a shooting star. The popular belief is that at the moment you see a shooting star, one soul is entering Heaven. Making the Sign of the Cross is a form of taking refuge in the Father, the Son, and the Holy Spirit. When you believe that something is the embodiment of evil, you hold out a cross to chase it away. In popular Buddhism, when people see something they think of as unwholesome, they invoke the name of Buddha. These are all practices of devotion. When you shine the light, darkness disappears. We may understand this as a kind of fight between light and darkness, but in reality, it is an embrace. Mindfulness, if practiced continuously, will be strong enough to embrace your fear or anger and transform it. We need not chase away evil. We can embrace and transform it in a nonviolent, nondualistic way.

TOUCHING THE LIVING CHRIST

When we invoke the Buddha's name, we evoke the same Buddha-qualities in ourselves. We practice in order to make the Buddha come alive within us, so we can be released from afflictions and attachments. But many people who invoke the name of Buddha do so without really trying to touch the Buddha seeds in themselves. There is a story of one woman who invoked the name of the Buddha hundreds of times a day without ever touching the essence of a Buddha. After practicing for ten years, she was still filled with anger and irritation. Her neighbor noticed this, and one day while she was practicing invoking the name of the Buddha, he knocked on her door and shouted, "Mrs. Ly, open the door!" She was so annoyed to be disturbed, she struck her bell very hard so that her neighbor would hear she was chanting and would stop disturbing her. But he kept calling, "Mrs. Ly, Mrs. Ly, Mrs. Ly, I need to speak with you." She became furious, threw her bell down on the ground, and stomped to the door, shouting, "Can't you see I'm invoking the name of the Buddha? Why are you bothering me now?" Her neighbor replied, "I only called your name twelve times, and look at how angry you have become. Imagine how angry the Buddha must be after you have been calling his name for ten years!"

Christians may do exactly as Mrs. Ly did if they only follow the rituals mechanically or pray without really being present. That is why they have been urged by Christian teachers to practice "The Prayer of the Heart." In Christianity, as well as in Buddhism, many people have little joy, ease, relaxation, release, or spaciousness of spirit in their practice. Even if they continue for one hundred years that way, they will not touch the living Buddha or the living Christ. If Christians who invoke the name of Jesus are only caught up in the words, they may lose sight of the life and teaching of Jesus. They practice only the form, not the essence. When you practice the essence, your mind becomes clear, and you attain joy. Christians who pray to God also have to learn deeply Christ's art of living if they want to enter His teachings. It is by watering the seeds of the awakened qualities that are already in us, by practicing mindfulness, that we touch the living Buddha and the living Christ.

∽

A MINI–PURE LAND

I became a monk at the age of sixteen in the tradition of Zen, but we also practiced Pure Land Buddhism in our temple. Pure Land Buddhism, which is very popular throughout East Asia, teaches people that if they practice well now, they will be reborn in the Western Paradise of the Buddha Amida, the Land of Wondrous Joy of the Buddha Aksobhya, or the Heaven of Gratitude of the Buddha Maitreya. A Pure Land is a land, perhaps in space and time, perhaps in our consciousness, where violence, hatred, craving, and discrimination have been reduced to a minimum because many people are practicing understanding and loving-kindness under the guidance of a Buddha and several bodhisattvas. Every practitioner of Buddha's way is, sooner or later, motivated by the desire to set up a Pure Land where he or she can share his or her joy, happiness, and practice with others. I myself have several times tried to set up a small Pure Land to share the practice of joy and peace with friends and students. In Vietnam it was Phuong Boi in the central highlands, and in France it is our Plum Village practice center. An ashram, such as the Community of the Arch in France, is also a Pure Land. A Great

Enlightened Being should be able to establish a great Pure Land. Others of us make the effort to begin a mini–Pure Land. This is only a natural tendency to share happiness.

A Pure Land is an ideal place for you to go to practice until you get fully enlightened. Many people in Asia practice recollection of the Buddha *(Buddhanusmrti),* reflecting on the qualities of the Buddha —visualizing him or invoking his name—in order to be reborn in his Pure Land. During the time of practice, they dwell in a kind of refuge in that Buddha. They are close to him, and they also water the seed of Buddhahood in themselves. But Pure Lands are impermanent. In Christianity, the Kingdom of God is the place you will go for eternity. But in Buddhism, the Pure Land is a kind of university where you practice with a teacher for a while, graduate, and then come back here to continue. Eventually, you discover that the Pure Land is in your own heart, that you do not need to go to a faraway place. You can set up your own mini–Pure Land, a Sangha of practice, right here, right now. But many people need to go away before they realize they do not have to go anywhere.

DEVOTIONAL AND TRANSFORMATIONAL PRACTICE

The practice of taking refuge can be done every day, several times a day. Whenever you feel agitated, sad, afraid, or worried, you can go back to your island of mindfulness. If you practice when you are not experiencing difficulty, it will be easier to go back to your island of self when the need is great. Don't wait until you are hit by a wave to go back to your island. Practice every day by living mindfully each moment of your life, and the practice will become a habit. Then when a difficult moment arrives, it will be natural and easy to take refuge. Walking, breathing, sitting, eating, and drinking tea in mindfulness are all practices of taking refuge. This is not a matter of belief. It is very grounded in experience. If I am ever in an airplane and the pilot announces that our plane is about to crash, I will practice mindful breathing and taking refuge in the island of self. I know that is the best thing I can do. If, down below, you know that I am practicing mindful breathing and taking refuge in the island of self, you will have confidence. I always practice walking meditation at airports. I try to leave for the airport early so that I will not have to rush when I am there. Mindful breathing unites body and mind. Many people call mindfulness the heart of Buddhist meditation. It is the first condition for touching anything deeply. When you practice mindfulness, you touch the Holy Spirit and become peaceful and solid.

Taking refuge in the Three Jewels is at the foundation of every Buddhist practice. Taking refuge in the Trinity is at the foundation of every Christian practice. Devotional and transformational practice may sound distinct, but devotional practice can also be transformational, and transformational practice requires devotion. Devotional practice relies more on the other, but there is also self-effort. Transformational practice relies on the self, but a community and a teacher are also necessary. Mindfulness and the Holy Spirit are at the heart of both.

NINE

THE OTHER SHORE

CONTINUATION

Recent polls show that nearly one-fourth of all Europeans and North Americans believe in some form of reincarnation. We seem to feel there must be a next life so that those who have acted improperly in this life will pay for their misdeeds. Or we feel that this earthly life is just too brief to be decisive for all of eternity. Or we are afraid that when we die we might be reduced to nothingness. So, revolting against the fact that we have to die, we prefer the idea of continuing with a new body, like changing our clothes. Will we continue or not after death? How? Where? When?

Reincarnation implies a re-entrance of the soul into the body. The third-century Christian theologian Origen taught about the pre-existence of the soul from all eternity before its incorporation into a body, a kind of "pre-incarnation." This idea is actually close to reincarnation, because if you are incarnated once, you might be incarnated twice, or more. The sixth-century Council of Constantinople condemned Origen for this teaching. Even today, most Christian leaders say the idea of reincarnation does not fit with Christianity. But resurrection does have to do with reincarnation. An immortal soul does not need to be resurrected. It is the body that does. According to the teaching of the Last Judgment, everyone will have his or her *body* resurrected. Elements of reincarnation are certainly present in the teachings of Christianity.

⁓

MANIFESTATION AND
REMANIFESTATION

At first, we might think of reincarnation as a soul entering a body. The body is seen as impermanent and the soul as permanent, and when we get rid of one body, we re-enter another. You may be surprised to know that people in Buddhist Asia are not fond of reincarnation. They want the circle of birth and death to end because they know it represents suffering without end. In popular Buddhism, reincarnation is accepted literally, without much examination, but as we continue to study and practice, the idea of an immortal soul gives way to another idea that is closer to reality. If we study the teachings of the Buddha and if we observe our own mind, we will find there is nothing permanent within the constituents of what we call our "self." The Buddha taught that a so-called "person" is really just five elements *(skandhas)* that come together for a limited period of time: our body, feelings, perceptions, mental states, and consciousness. These five elements are, in fact, changing all the time. Not a single element remains the same for two consecutive moments.

Not only is our body impermanent, but our so-called soul is also impermanent. It, too, is comprised only of elements like feelings, perceptions, mental states, and consciousness. When the idea of an *immortal* soul is replaced, our understanding of reincarnation gets closer to the truth. The idea of reincarnation is somehow still there, but our understanding is different. We see that there are only rapidly changing constituents.

In Buddhism, we do not actually use the word "reincarnation." We say "rebirth." But even rebirth is problematic. According to the teachings of the Buddha, "birth" does not exist either. Birth generally means from nothing you become something, and death generally means from something you become nothing. But if we observe the things around us, we find that nothing comes from nothing. Before its so-called birth, this flower already existed in other forms—clouds, sunshine, seeds, soil, and many other elements. Rather than birth and rebirth, it is more accurate to say "manifestation" *(vijñapti)* and "remanifestation." The so-called birthday of the flower is really a day of its remanifestation. It has already been here in other forms, and now it has made an effort to remanifest. Manifestation means its constituents have always been here in some form, and now, since conditions are sufficient, it is capable of manifesting itself as a flower. When things have manifested, we commonly say that they are born, but in fact, they are not. When conditions are no longer sufficient and the flower ceases to manifest, we say the flower has died, but that is not correct either. Its constituents have merely transformed themselves into other elements, like compost and soil. We have to transcend notions like birth, death, being, and non-being. Reality is free from all notions.

∾

TRUE FAITH
IS ALIVE

In the beginning, we might have embarked upon the path of Buddhism thanks to a belief in reincarnation, but as we continue to practice and touch reality, our beliefs change. We needn't be afraid of this. In the course of our study and practice, as we touch reality more and more deeply, our beliefs naturally evolve and become more solid. When our beliefs are based on our own direct experience of reality and not on notions offered by others, no one can remove these beliefs from us. Making a long-term commitment to a concept is much more dangerous. If ten years pass without the growth of our belief, one day we will wake up and discover that we can no longer believe in what we did. The notion of ten years ago is no longer sound or adequate, and we are plunged into the darkness of disbelief.

Our faith must be alive. It cannot be just a set of rigid beliefs and notions. Our faith must evolve every day and bring us joy, peace, freedom, and love. Faith implies practice, living our daily life in mindfulness. Some people think that prayer or meditation involves only our minds or our hearts. But we also have to pray with our bodies, with our actions in the world. And our actions must be modelled after those of the living Buddha or the living Christ. If we live as they did, we will have deep understanding and pure actions, and we will do our share to help create a more peaceful world for our children and all of the children of God.

∞

EACH MOMENT IS A
MOMENT OF RENEWAL

All of us possess the energy of mindfulness, the energy of the Holy Spirit, only its intensity and strength vary in each person. Our daily practice is to increase, to strengthen that power. There is no need to wait until Easter to celebrate. When the Holy Spirit is present, Jesus is already here. He does not have to be resurrected. We can feel Him right now. It is not a matter of reincarnation, rebirth, or even resurrection. Dwelling mindfully, we know that each moment is a moment of renewal. I wish I could be like Asita and Simeon, the holy men who came to see the Buddha and Jesus, and tell you how important your birth is.

❦

ENLIGHTENMENT GROWS

Several years ago, after practicing walking meditation with three children in Switzerland, I asked them, "Do you think the enlightenment of the Buddha can grow?" They answered, "Yes," and I was very happy. The children affirmed something I also believe, that enlightenment is alive, like a tree. If it does not continue to grow, it will die. The enlightenment of the Buddha, the compassion and loving-kindness of Jesus, grow every day. We ourselves are responsible for their growth. Our bodies are the continuation of the Buddha's body. Our compassion and understanding are the compassion and understanding of Jesus. Awareness is the Buddha in person. If we live mindfully, we encounter the Buddha and Jesus Christ all the time.

❧

NIRVANA IS AVAILABLE NOW

Some waves on the ocean are high and some are low. Waves appear to be born and to die. But if we look more deeply, we see that the waves, although coming and going, are also water, which is always there. Notions like high and low, birth and death can be applied to waves, but water is free of such distinctions. Enlightenment for a wave is the moment the wave realizes that it is water. At that moment, all fear of death disappears. If you practice deeply, one day you will realize that you are free from birth and death, free from many of the dangers that have been assaulting you. When you see that, you will have no trouble building a boat that can carry you across the waves of birth and death. Smiling, you will understand that you do not have to abandon this world in order to be free. You will know that nirvana, the Kingdom of Heaven, is available here and now.

The Buddha seldom talked about this because he knew that if he talked about nirvana, we would spend too much time talking about it and not practicing. But he did make a few rare statements, such as this one from *Udana* viii, 3: "Verily, there is an unborn, unoriginated, uncreated, unformed. If

there were not this unborn, unoriginated, uncreated, unformed, then an escape from the world of
the born, the originated, the created, and the
formed would not be possible." Early Buddhism did
not have the ontological flavor we find in later
Buddhism. The Buddha dealt more with the phenomenal world. His teaching was very practical.
Theologians spend a lot of time, ink, and breath
talking about God. This is exactly what the Buddha
did not want his disciples to do, because he wanted
them to have time to practice samatha (stopping,
calming), vipasyana (looking deeply), taking refuge
in the Three Jewels, the Five Precepts, and so on.

THE EXTINCTION OF NOTIONS

The philosopher Ludwig Wittgenstein said,
"Concerning that which cannot be talked about, we
should not say anything." We cannot talk about it,
but we can experience it. We can experience the
non-born, non-dying, non-beginning, non-ending
because it is reality itself. The way to experience it is
to abandon our habit of perceiving everything
through concepts and representations. Theologians
have spent thousands of years talking about God as
one representation. This is called onto-theology,

and it is talking about what we should not talk about.

Protestant theologian Paul Tillich said that God is not a person, but also not less than a person. Whether we speak of God as not a person, as a non-person, as not less than a person, or as more than a person, these attributes do not mean very much. One flower is made of the whole cosmos. We cannot say that the flower is less than this or more than that. When we extinguish our ideas of more and less, is and is not, we attain the extinction of ideas and notions, which in Buddhism is called nirvana. The ultimate dimension of reality has nothing to do with concepts. It is not just absolute reality that cannot be talked about. Nothing can be conceived or talked about. Take, for instance, a glass of apple juice. You cannot talk about apple juice to someone who has never tasted it. No matter what you say, the other person will not have the true experience of apple juice. The only way is to drink it. It is like a turtle telling a fish about life on dry land. You cannot describe dry land to a fish. He could never understand how one might be able to breathe without water. Things cannot be described by concepts and words. They can only be encountered by direct experience.

≪

MORE TIME FOR YOUR TEA

Wittgenstein's statement, "Concerning that which cannot be talked about, we should not say anything," might lead you to think there are things we can talk about and things we cannot. But, in fact, nothing can be talked about, perceived, or described by representation. If you talk about things you have not experienced, you are wasting your and other people's time. As you continue the practice of looking deeply, you will see this more and more clearly, and you will save a lot of paper and publishing enterprises and have more time to enjoy your tea and live your daily life in mindfulness.

Rohitassa asked the Buddha whether it is possible to get out of this world of birth and death by traveling, and the Buddha said no, not even if you were to travel at the speed of light. But he did not say it is impossible to transcend the world of birth and death. He said that we only need to look deeply into our body to touch the world of no-birth and no-death. But we cannot just talk about it. We have to practice, to experience it in our own being. The world of no-birth and no-death is not something apart from the world of birth and death. In fact, they are identical.

❧

THE OTHER SHORE IS
THIS SHORE

When the Buddha spoke of salvation or emancipation, he used the word *parayana,* "the other shore." The other shore represents the realm of no-birth, no-death, and no suffering. Sometimes the concept "other shore" is not clear enough, so the Buddha also used the word *tathata,* which means "reality as it is." We cannot talk about it, we cannot conceive it. Sometimes we call it nirvana, the extinction of all words, ideas, and concepts. When the concept "other shore" is misunderstood, nirvana comes to the rescue. When we think of another shore, we may think that it is completely different from this shore, that to reach it we have to abandon this shore completely. The true teaching is that the other shore is this very shore. In all schools of Buddhism, the teaching of no-coming, no-going, no-being, no-nonbeing, no-birth, and no-death exists. Mahayana Buddhists remind us that this teaching is only a finger pointing to the moon. It is not the moon itself.

EVERYTHING CAN BE SPIRITUAL

Jesus pointed to that same reality of no-birth, no-death. He called it the Kingdom of God. The Kingdom of God is not something distinct from God, whom he called *Abba,* "Father." Just as the concept "other shore" can create the misunderstanding that the other shore is not this shore, the concept "Father" can also be misleading. For instance, feminists in our time ask why "Father" and not "Mother"? Eternal life is the kind of life that includes death. In fact, eternal life without death is not possible. It is like two sides of a coin. Eternal life is the whole coin. Noneternal life is just one side of the coin. Once you choose eternal life, you choose death as well, and both are life. But if you want to take only one side of the coin, you have no coin.

Theology has gone a long way trying to describe "God" or the "Kingdom of God," that wonderful reality that, in fact, cannot be talked about. Over many centuries, theology has thus become metaphysical theology or onto-theology to such an extent that we neglect the true teaching of Jesus concerning the way to live that reality. Since German philosopher Martin Heidegger, theologians have been trying to go back to the beginning and have been more careful in making statements about God.

Many people in our time want to go back to Jesus and His teaching. Sometimes terms like "secular Christianity" or "atheistic Christianity" are used to describe this movement. There are those who worry that secular or atheistic Christianity is no longer real Christianity. To me, if you live deeply the teaching of Jesus, everything you say and do in your daily life will be deeply spiritual. I would not call it secular or atheistic at all. Suppose we do not celebrate a Eucharist in a church, but sit together in the open air to share our bread, eating it mindfully and gratefully, aware of the marvelous nature of the bread. Such an act cannot be described as secular or atheistic.

TOUCHING THE LIVING BUDDHA

God as the ground of being cannot be conceived of. Nirvana also cannot be conceived of. If we are aware when we use the word "nirvana" or the word "God" that we are talking about the ground of being, there is no danger in using these words. But if we say, "According to Buddhism, this exists," or, "This does not exist," it is not Buddhism, because the ideas of being and non-being are extremes that the Buddha transcended. When we share the Dharma, we must speak carefully so that we and our listeners do not get stuck in words or concepts. It is our duty to transcend words and concepts to be able to encounter reality. To be in touch with the source of our own wisdom is the most eloquent way to show that Buddhism is alive. We can touch the living Buddha. We can also touch the living Christ. When we see someone overflowing with love and understanding, someone who is keenly aware of what is going on, we know that they are very close to the Buddha and to Jesus Christ.

∞

TREES AND BIRDS PREACHING THE DHARMA

The Buddha is often described as having "three bodies": Dharmakaya, Sambhogakaya, and Nirmanakaya. Dharmakaya is the embodiment of the Dharma, always shining, always enlightening trees, grass, birds, human beings, and so on, always emitting light. It is this Buddha who is preaching now and not just 2,500 years ago. Sometimes we call this

Buddha Vairochana, the ontological Buddha, the Buddha at the center of the universe.

The Sambhogakaya is the body of bliss. Because the Buddha practices mindfulness, he has immeasurable peace, joy, and happiness, and that is why we can touch his body of bliss, sometimes called the body of enjoyment or body of rewards. The Sambhogakaya represents the peace and happiness of the Buddha, the fruit of his practice. When you practice mindfulness, you enjoy within you the fruit of the practice. You are happy and peaceful, and your happiness and peace radiate around you for others to enjoy. When you do this, you are sending many Sambhogakayas into the world to help relieve the suffering of living beings. Each of us has the capacity of transforming many living beings if we know how to cultivate the seed of enlightenment within ourselves.

Shakyamuni, the historical Buddha, is the Nirmanakaya, the transformation body, a light ray sent by the sun of the Dharmakaya. Those in touch with Vairochana are also in touch with Shakyamuni. But if that ray is not apparent to us, we do not need to worry. The sun is still there. If we cannot listen directly to Shakyamuni, if we are open enough we can listen to Vairochana. In addition, many other transformation Buddhas are also expounding the same Dharma—the trees, the birds, the violet bamboo, and the yellow chrysanthemums are all preaching the Dharma that Shakyamuni taught 2,500 years ago. We can be in touch with him through any of these. He is a living Buddha, always available.

In Christianity, mystery is often described as darkness. When Victor Hugo lost his daughter, he complained, "Man sees only one side of things, the other side is plunged into the night of frightening mystery." In many Buddhist sutras, everyone in the assembly experiences bliss when they are touched by the beams of light emanating from the Buddha. In Buddhism, the word *"avidya,"* ignorance, means literally "the lack of light." *Vidya,* understanding, is made of light.

∞

RINSING THE MOUTH, WASHING THE EARS

In the Greek Orthodox church, theologians talk about "apophatic theology," or "negative theology." "Apophatic" is from the Greek *apophasis,* which means "denying." You say that God is not this, God is not that, until you get rid of all your concepts of God. The second-century Buddhist philosopher Nagarjuna developed a similar dialectic to remove our ideas concerning reality. He did not describe reality, because reality is what it is and cannot be described. Buddhism teaches us that reality is quite different from our concepts. The reality of a table is quite different from the concept "table." Every word we use has a concept behind it. The word "God" is based on a concept of "God." According to Buddhism, meditation on a rabbit's horns or a tortoise's hair, things we do not believe exist, can also lead to enlightenment. These concepts are comprised of real elements that we can merge in our imagination. We have an image of horns and an image of rabbit, so why not have a rabbit with horns? The concept "rabbit's horn" is a true concept, as real as any other concept.

One Buddhist teacher said that every time he pronounced the word "Buddhism," he had to rinse his mouth out three times. Even the word "Buddhism" can cause misunderstanding. People may think of Buddhism as something that can exist by itself, independent of Christianity, Judaism, or anything else. Rinsing his mouth was a kind of preventive medicine to remind himself (and his students) not to cling to the concept "Buddhism" as something that can exist all by itself. One day someone in the congregation stood up and said, "Teacher, every time I hear you pronounce the word 'Buddhism,' I have to go to the river and wash my ears three times!" The teacher approved that statement. In Buddhist circles, we are careful to avoid getting stuck in concepts, even the concepts "Buddhism" and "Buddha." If you think of the Buddha as someone separate from the rest of the world, you will never recognize a Buddha even if you see him on the street. That is why one Zen Master said to his student, "When you meet the Buddha, kill him!" He meant that the student should kill the *Buddha-concept* in order for him to experience the *real Buddha* directly.

Another Zen teacher said, "To end suffering, you must touch the world of no-birth and no-death." His student asked, "Where is the world of no-birth and no-death?" The master replied, "It is right here in the world of birth and death." The world of impermanence and non-self *is* the world of birth and death. The world of nirvana is also the world of birth and death. Salvation is possible. It is possible to enter the world of no-birth and no-death through the practice of living each moment of your life in awareness. Jewish theologian Abraham Heschel said that to live by the Torah, the Jewish law, is to live the life of eternity within time. We live in the historical dimension and yet touch the ultimate dimension. But if we talk too much about it, we move far from the ultimate dimension. That is why in Zen Buddhist circles people are urged to experience and not to talk a lot.

∾

THE HOLY SPIRIT CAN
BE IDENTIFIED

In every school of Christianity, we see people who follow the same spirit, who do not want to speculate on what cannot be speculated about. "Negative theology" is an effort and practice to prevent Christians from being caught by notions and concepts that prevent them from touching the living spirit of Christianity. When we speak of negative theology, the theology of the Death of God, we are talking about the death of every concept we may have of God in order to experience God as a living reality directly.

A good theologian is one who says almost nothing about God, even though the word "theology" means "discourse about God." It is risky to talk about God. The notion of God might be an obstacle for us to touch God as love, wisdom, and mindfulness. The Buddha was very clear about this. He said, "You tell me that you are in love with a beautiful woman, but when I ask you, 'What is the color of her eyes? What is her name? What is the name of her town?' you cannot tell me. I don't believe you are really in love with something real." Your notion of God may be vague like that, not having to do with reality. The Buddha was not against God. He was only against notions of God that are mere mental constructions that do not correspond to reality, notions that prevent us from developing ourselves and touching ultimate reality. That is why I believe it is safer to approach God through the Holy Spirit than through the door of theology. We can identify the Holy Spirit whenever it makes its presence felt. Whenever we see someone who is loving, compassionate, mindful, caring, and understanding, we know that the Holy Spirit is there.

∞

TOUCHING THE ULTIMATE DIMENSION

One day as I was about to step on a dry leaf, I saw the leaf in the ultimate dimension. I saw that it was not really dead, but that it was merging with the moist soil in order to appear on the tree the following spring in another form. I smiled at the leaf and said, "You are pretending." Everything is pretending to be born and pretending to die, including that leaf.

The Buddha said, "When conditions are sufficient, the body reveals itself, and we say the body exists. When conditions are not sufficient, the body cannot be perceived by us, and we say the body does not exist." The day of our "death" is a day of our continuation in many other forms. If you know how to touch your ancestors in the ultimate dimension, they will always be there with you. If you touch your own hand, face, or hair and look very deeply, you can see that they are there in you, smiling. This is a deep practice. The ultimate dimension is a state of coolness, peace, and joy. It is not a state to be attained after you "die." You can touch the ultimate dimension right now by breathing, walking, and drinking your tea in mindfulness. Everything and everyone is dwelling in nirvana, in the Kingdom of God. A farmer looking at his land in winter can already see his crop, because he knows that all of the conditions are there—land, seeds, water, fertilizer, farm equipment, and so on—except one, warm weather, and that will come in a matter of months. So it would be inaccurate to say his crop does not exist. It *is* already there. It needs only one more condition to manifest. When St. Francis asked the almond tree to tell him about God, in just a few seconds the tree was covered with beautiful flowers.

St. Francis was standing on the side of the ultimate dimension. It was winter. There were no leaves, flowers, or fruits, but he saw the flowers.

We are entirely capable of touching the ultimate dimension. When we touch one thing with deep awareness, we touch everything. Touching the present moment, we realize that the present is made of the past and is creating the future. When we drink a cup of tea very deeply, we touch the whole of time. To meditate, to live a life of prayer, is to live each moment of life deeply. Through meditation and prayer, we see that waves are made only of water, that the historical and the ultimate dimensions are one. Even while living in the world of waves, we touch the water, knowing that a wave is nothing but water. We suffer if we touch only the waves, but if we learn how to stay in touch with the water, we feel the greatest relief. Touching nirvana, touching the Kingdom of God, liberates us from many worries. We enter a spiritual practice seeking relief in the historical dimension. We calm our body and mind and establish our stillness, our freshness, and our solidity. We practice loving-kindness, concentration, and transforming our anger, and we feel some relief. But when we touch the ultimate dimension of reality, we get the deepest kind of relief.

Each of us has the capacity to touch nirvana and be free from birth and death, one and many, coming and going.

Christian contemplation includes the practice of resting in God, which, I believe, is the equivalent of touching nirvana. Although God cannot be described by using concepts and notions, that does not mean you cannot experience God the Father. If the wave does not have to die to become water, then we do not have to die to enter the Kingdom of God. The Kingdom of God is available here and now. The energy of the Holy Spirit is the energy that helps us touch the Kingdom of God. Tillich has said that speaking of God as a person is just a figure of speech. He said that God is the ground of being. This makes me think of the water that is the ground of being for the wave. He also said that God is the ultimate reality, and that makes me remember nirvana. I do not think there is that much difference between Christians and Buddhists. Most of the boundaries we have created between our two traditions are artificial. Truth has no boundaries. Our differences may be mostly differences in emphasis.

You are born in your tradition, and naturally you become a Buddhist or a Christian. Buddhism or Christianity is part of your culture and civilization.

You are familiar with your culture and appreciate the good things in it. You may not be aware that in other cultures and civilizations there are values that people are attached to. If you are open enough, you will understand that your tradition does not contain all truths and values. It is easy to get caught in the idea that salvation is not possible outside of your tradition. A deep and correct practice of your tradition may release you from that dangerous belief.

In the Gospel according to Matthew, the Kingdom of God is described as a mustard seed. "The Kingdom of Heaven is like a mustard seed that someone took and sowed in the field. It is the smallest of all the seeds, but when it has grown it is the greatest of shrubs and becomes a tree so that the birds of the air come and make nests in its branches." What is that seed? Where is the soil? What is it if not our own consciousness? We hear repeatedly that God is within us. To me, it means that God is within our consciousness. Buddha nature, the seed of mindfulness, is in the soil of our consciousness. It may be small, but if we know how to care for it, how to touch it, how to water it moment after moment, it becomes an important refuge for all the birds of the air. It has the power of transforming everything. In Buddhist practice, we learn how to touch that seed in every moment, how to help it grow, how to make it into the light that can guide us.

In the Gospel according to Matthew, the Kingdom of Heaven is also described as yeast: "The Kingdom of Heaven is like yeast that a woman took and mixed in with three measures of flour until all of it was leavened." A little yeast has the power to leaven a lot of flour. The flour is our consciousness. Inside that consciousness are negative seeds: seeds of fear, hatred, and confusion. But if you have the seed of the Kingdom of God inside and know how to touch it, it will have the power to leaven, to transform everything.

∽

TOUCHING THE WATER WITHIN THE WAVES

The Kingdom of God is also said to be like a treasure that someone finds and hides in a field. Then, in his joy, he sells all he has and buys that field. If you are capable of touching that treasure, you know that nothing can be compared to it. It is the source of true joy, true peace, and true happiness. Once you have touched it, you realize that all the things you have considered to be conditions for

your happiness are nothing. They may even be obstacles for your own happiness, and you can get rid
of them without regret. We are all looking for the
conditions for our own happiness, and we know
what things have made us suffer. But we have not
yet seen or touched the treasure of happiness. When
we touch it, even once, we know that we have the
capacity of letting go of everything else.

That treasure of happiness, the Kingdom of
Heaven, may be called the ultimate dimension of
reality. When you see only waves, you might miss
the water. But if you are mindful, you will be able to
touch the water within the waves as well. Once you
are capable of touching the water, you will not mind
the coming and going of the waves. You are no
longer concerned about the birth and the death of
the wave. You are no longer afraid. You are no
longer upset about the beginning or the end of the
wave, or that the wave is higher or lower, more or
less beautiful. You are capable of letting these ideas
go because you have already touched the water.

TEN

FAITH AND PRACTICE

PENETRATING THE HEART OF REALITY

Our faith must be alive, always growing, like a tree. It is our true religious experience that nourishes our faith and allows it to grow. In the Buddhist tradition, religious experience is described as awakening (bodhi) or insight (prajña). It is not intellectual, not made of notions and concepts, but of the kind of understanding that brings more solidity, freedom, joy, and faith. For genuine awakening to be possible, we must let go of notions and concepts about nirvana, and about God. We must let go not just of our notions and concepts about the ultimate but also of our notions and concepts about things in the phenomenal realm. In Buddhist practice, we contemplate impermanence, non-self, emptiness, and interbeing to help us touch the phenomenal world more deeply, release our notions and concepts about things, and penetrate the heart of reality. When we touch "things-in-themselves," we see that they are quite different from our notions and concepts about them. Our notions and concepts are the result of wrong perceptions. That is why, in order to have direct access to their reality, we have to abandon all of our wrong perceptions. When nuclear scientists want to enter the world of elementary particles, they too must abandon their notions of things and objects. French scientist Alfred Kastler said, "Objects or things that have always been thought of as constituents of nature must be renounced." In the same way, we must abandon our notions of God, Buddha, nirvana, self, non-self, birth, death, being, and non-being.

❦

ONLY THE SON AND THE
HOLY SPIRIT KNOW HIM

Letting go of notions and concepts may seem to be difficult, but that is exactly what Buddhist meditation teaches us to do. We can use any of a variety of methods to accomplish this. In the beginning, we sometimes use new notions and concepts to neutralize our old ones and lead us to direct experience of reality. The notion of emptiness *(sunyata),* for example, can liberate us from the belief in a self. But then, if we are not vigilant, we can get caught in the notion of emptiness, which is even a bigger problem. To give us a second chance, the Buddha offered the notion of non-emptiness *(asunyata).* If we are able to see that emptiness and non-emptiness point to the same reality, both notions will be transcended and we will touch the world that is free from notions and concepts.

Christians understand that God cannot be experienced through notions and concepts. They speak of "the incomprehensibility of God." Saint John Chrysostom wrote, "Let us invoke Him as the inexpressible God, incomprehensible, invisible, and unknowable. Let us avow that He surpasses all power of human speech, that He eludes the grasp of every mortal intelligence, that the angels cannot penetrate Him, nor the seraphim see Him in full clarity, nor the cherubim fully understand Him. For He is invisible to the principalities and powers, the virtues of all creatures without exception, only the Son and the Holy Spirit know Him." "Only the Son and the Holy Spirit know Him" because they represent nonconceptual knowing. The Son and the Holy Spirit have direct access to God because they are free from ideas and images of God.

This nonconceptual nature of God is often described by Christians as the mystical night. Saint Gregory of Nyssa, of the Eastern Orthodox church, wrote, "Night designates the contemplation of invisible things after the manner of Moses, who entered into the darkness where God was, this God who makes of darkness His hiding place. Surrounded by the living night the soul seeks Him who is hidden in darkness. She possesses indeed the love of Him whom she seeks, but the beloved escapes the grasp of her thoughts." God the Father and the Kingdom of God must be the objects of our daily *experience*. If Christian monks, nuns, laymen, and laywomen do not touch God the Father in their daily lives, their "primitive images" of God will, one day, no longer sustain their joy, peace, and happiness.

∽

THE SUBSTANCE OF
FAITH

When you begin to practice, you need some tools, just as someone who comes to work on a farm needs tools to work the soil. When you are given tools, there is no use in having them and not working the soil. With proper instruction, you can learn how to handle your tools and how to work the soil. Certain ideas and images can be accepted as tools of spiritual practice. By using them, you can acquire some peace, comfort, stability, and joy. If you continue the practice and make some progress, more sophisticated images and ideas will be provided. These are tools to help you explore the soil of your own life. The Buddha described the practice as *citta bhavana,* cultivating the mind and heart.

After practicing for some time, one day you will find that the images and ideas you have been using are no longer of help, and it is necessary at that point to abandon all ideas and images in order to obtain a truly deep realization. This genuine experience or insight is the very substance of faith, the kind of faith that no one can remove from you because it is not made of images, ideas, or dogma. You cannot be tempted to doubt God or nirvana because God or nirvana has become the object and subject of your own true experience. For this to happen, two things are essential: first, you have to practice for your belief to become true experience; second, the practice should not be abandoned after some stability and peace have been obtained. We shall examine the reasons for this shortly.

∞

TAKING REFUGE

Many Buddhists invoke the holy names of Shakyamuni Buddha, Amitabha Buddha, and Avalokitesvara Bodhisattva. While invoking these holy names, the practitioners' minds should be filled with the wholesome qualities of these Buddhas and bodhisattvas. This is the secret of success in the practice known as "Recollection of the Buddha" *(Buddhanusmrti)*. There are also other ways of practicing Buddhanusmrti, such as visualizing, reciting the Ten Names of the Buddha, meditating on the wisdom and the compassionate actions of the Buddhas, and so forth. The practitioner may chant, "The Lord is Arhat. He is the perfectly enlightened. He is endowed with knowledge and action. He is happy, the knower of all worlds, the insurmountable charioteer of men to be tamed, the teacher of gods and men, the Buddha, the Blessed One."

Buddhists also practice the Recollection of the Dharma *(Dharmanusmrti)*. The living Dharma is the way embodied by Buddhas, bodhisattvas, and all who practice it. The practitioner recites and contemplates, "The Dharma has been well proclaimed by the Buddha. It brings justice right in this life. It brings coolness and removes the flames of passion and craving. It is timeless. It brings us to a wholesome end. It says, 'Come and see for yourself.' It is recognizable by the wise ones." Or they may chant, "Homage to the *Lotus Sutra*," and similar practices.

To practice the Recollection of the Sangha *(Sanghanusmrti)*, Buddhists recite and contemplate, "Well attained is the Order of the Blessed One's disciples. Upright is the Order of the Blessed One's disciples. Righteous and Dharma-abiding is the Order of the Blessed One's disciples. The Sangha is comprised of the four pairs and the eight types who are worthy of offerings, hospitality, gifts, and salutations, unsurpassable fields of merit in the world." All Buddhists practice taking refuge in the Three Jewels: Buddha, Dharma, and Sangha. Doing so brings the feeling of calm, solidity, and comfort, and nourishes faith. "I take refuge in the Buddha. I take refuge in the Dharma. I take refuge in the Sangha. *(Buddham*

saranam gacchami. Dharmam saranam gacchami.
Sangham saranam gacchami.)''

⚭

INTERIOR RECOLLECTION

In the Christian tradition, prayer produces a similar effect. Prayers are drawn from the Bible, especially the Psalms, and these words become the words of the practitioner through memorizing and repeating them with concentration. Christian meditation often takes scriptures as its object, *meditatio scripturarum*. The meditator puts all his or her heart into this practice of prayer and meditation. That is why it is called Prayer of the Heart.

Like their Buddhist counterparts, Christian practitioners do not engage in excessive intellectual or analytical scrutiny of the scriptures. For the Desert Fathers, prayer was minimally wordy. Saint Macarius said, "It is not necessary to use many words. Only stretch out your arms and say, 'Lord, have pity on me as you desire and as you well know how.' And if the enemy presses you hard, say, 'Lord, come to my aid.' " Other early Christian monks also urged people to use short, simple prayers drawn from the Psalms. The most frequently used was "O God, come to my assistance. *(Deus in adjutorium meum intende.)*"

Christians also practice reciting the holy name of Jesus Christ. Saint Macarius said, "There is no other perfect meditation than the saving and blessed name of our Lord Jesus Christ dwelling without interruption in you." This practice is called by Christians "interior recollection" (equivalent to the Sanskrit *anusmrti,* and the Pali *anussati).* The practice consists of abandoning distracting thoughts and humbly invoking the name of Jesus with all your heart. Thomas Merton wrote, "This simple practice is considered to be of crucial importance in the monastic prayer of the Eastern Church, since the sacramental power of the name of Jesus is believed to bring the Holy Spirit into the heart of the praying monk."

For the monks of old, the secret of success in the practice was to keep the name of Jesus always in mind. The name of Jesus brings the energy of God, namely the Holy Spirit, into your own being. When the monk was able to do this, he could live his daily life in the presence of God. Buddhists in the Pure Land tradition practice similarly. They know what is most essential is to maintain true concentration while reciting the name of Buddha, just as Christians know that they have to practice with their hearts and not call the Lord's name in vain.

∞

AFFLICTIONS BLOCK
THE WAY

Christians emphasize Prayer of the Heart, and Buddhists speak about one-pointed mind *(cittaseka-gata)*. Christians and Buddhists both realize that without concentration, without abandoning distracting thoughts, prayer and meditation will not bear fruit. Concentration and devotion bring calm, peace, stability, and comfort to both Buddhists and Christians. If farmers use farming tools to cultivate their land, practitioners use prayer and meditation to cultivate their consciousness. The fruits and flowers of the practice spring forth from the soil of the mind.

Buddhists and Christians know that nirvana or the Kingdom of God is within their hearts. Buddhist sutras speak of Buddha nature as the seed of enlightenment that is already in everyone's consciousness. The Gospels speak of the Kingdom of God as a mustard seed planted in the soil of consciousness. The practices of prayer and meditation help us touch the most valuable seeds that are within us, and they put us in contact with the ground of our being. Buddhists consider nirvana, or the ultimate dimension of reality, as the ground of being. The original mind, according to Buddhism, is always shining. Afflictions such as craving, anger, doubt, fear, and forgetfulness are what block the light, so the practice is to remove these five hindrances. When the energy of mindfulness is present, transformation takes place. When the energy of the Holy Spirit is within you, understanding, love, peace, and stability are possible. God is within. You are, yet you are not, but God is in you. This is interbeing. This is non-self.

But I am afraid that many Christians and many Buddhists do not practice, or if they do, they practice only when they find themselves in difficult situations, and after that, they forget. Or their practice may be superficial. They support churches and temples, organize ceremonies, convert people, do charity work or social work, or take up an apostolic ministry, but do not practice mindfulness or pray while they act. They may devote an hour each day for chanting and liturgy, but after a while, the practice becomes dry and automatic and they do not know how to refresh it. They may believe that they are serving the Buddha, the Dharma, the Sangha, or serving the Trinity and the church, but their practice does not touch the living Buddha or the living Christ. At the same time, these men and women do not hesitate to align themselves with those in power in order to strengthen the position of their church or community. They believe that political power is needed for the well-being of their church or community. They build up a self instead of letting go of the ideas of self. Then they look at this self as absolute truth and dismiss all other spiritual traditions as false. This is a very dangerous attitude; it always leads to conflicts and war. Its nature is intolerance.

∞

THE ABYSS
OF DOUBT

Another danger of the lack of authentic, regular practice and the lack of spiritual maturation is that one day the believer will fall into the abyss of doubt. When suffering, fear, and doubt come together in an intensive way, the prayer that worked a little many years earlier may no longer be effective. The ideas, images, and analogies that were invoked in the past may not be able to cover over the vast interior emptiness. The Diamond Sutra teaches that the Tathagata cannot be seen through sounds or images. Christian mystics teach that God is invisible, unknowable, and free from mental representation. If we do not continue to grow, we will not be able to touch the reality of the absolute. That is why it is crucial to remember that the practice should not be abandoned after some stability and peace have been attained.

One day when you are plunged into the dark night of doubt, the images and notions that were helpful in the beginning no longer help. They only cover up the anguish and suffering that have begun to surface. Thomas Merton wrote, "The most crucial aspect of this experience is precisely the temptation to doubt God Himself." This is a genuine risk. If you stick to an idea or an image of God and if you do not touch the reality of God, one day you will be plunged into doubt. According to Merton, "Here we are advancing beyond the stage where God made Himself accessible to our mind in simple and primitive images." Simple and primitive images may have been the object of our faith in God in the beginning, but as we advance, He becomes present without any image, beyond any satisfactory mental representation. We come to a point where any notion we had can no longer represent God.

∞

THE ORIGINAL MIND

In the Buddhist monastic tradition, monks are urged not to live too comfortably. A life that is too comfortable will make spiritual growth difficult. Food, clothing, and lodging should always be adequate, but not excessive. A layperson who wants to practice the Way should also live a simple life. Jesus said that it is as difficult for a wealthy person to enter the Kingdom of God as it is for a camel to go through the eye of a needle. Christian monastic prayers flourish in environments like deserts, where there is not a lot of comfort. Thomas Merton wrote, "We must frankly admit that self-denial and sacrifice are absolutely essential to the life of prayer." I understand him, although I would not describe a simple life, a life free of craving, as self-denial or sacrifice. A life of prayer and contemplation can be filled with joy and happiness.

Without continuous and deep practice, monks can also be caught by the traps of the world. The activity of a contemplative monk should be contemplation. In the Sutra on the Full Awareness of Breathing (Anapanasati Sutta), the Buddha took a deep look at the community of monks who had been practicing at the Jeta Grove and declared, "My friends, I am very happy to see that you have been doing the most important thing that a monk should do, which is to practice." It was recorded in this sutra that not only did the senior monks practice well during the retreat but they also took good care of the young monks and helped guide their practice. That brought great happiness to the Buddha. The task of a monk is to practice and not to take care of the worldly life. If we are not careful enough, teaching the Dharma or performing apostolic ministry will carry us away from our original mind, the mind of practice, the mind of love, which is the most precious possession a monk can have.

∽

AN EXPRESSION
OF LOVE

Buddhists call original mind, the mind of enlightenment, *bodhicitta*. Saint Gregory taught that the contemplative life is the heavenly life, which cannot be lived "in this world." Monks need to avoid doing secular business. To penetrate the mystery of God, the contemplative must "rest from exterior action and cleave only to the desire of the Maker." In the Middle Ages, many monks followed this teaching.

The vocation of the monk was to stay in the monastery and pray. When he was called forth to engage in church affairs, he was expected to do so with weeping and lamentation. Saint Peter of Celles, a twelfth-century Benedictine monk, said that "episcopal [i.e., bishops'] business" is simply "the world."

Is it possible for an apostolic ministry to go together with a contemplative life? In both Buddhist and Christian circles, the answer is yes, it is possible, but not easy. To succeed, we need support, and the most important support is the presence of others who are capable of living the contemplative life while doing the work that needs to be done. Our work is performed as an expression of love. We cannot avoid it, so we should do it in a way that allows a contemplative life to be possible.

In the fourth century, Saint Basil taught that an active religious life is possible. Ascetics, he said, should maintain contact with the world, or at least with the Christian community, and take care of charity and mercy works. The monk's private prayer is the prayer carried on while he is at work. Saint Basil said, "For prayer and psalmody every hour is suitable, that while one's hands are busy with their tasks we may praise God sometimes with the tongue, or if not, with the heart. . . . Thus we acquire a recollected spirit, when in every action we beg from God the success of our labor and satisfy our debt of gratitude to Him.''

∾

HOW NOT TO LOSE
THE CONTEMPLATIVE LIFE

The Sutra on the Four Establishments of Mindfulness *(Satipatthana Sutta)*, one of the most basic texts of Buddhist meditation, teaches that mindfulness must be practiced throughout the day, in whatever position you find yourself and during whatever action you undertake. Mindfulness practice is not confined to the sitting position. The monk practices mindfulness while putting on his robe, washing his bowl, walking, standing, bending, stretching, carrying water, splitting wood, and so on. Based on this teaching, engaged Buddhism was practiced by the monks in Vietnam during the war in the 1960s and 1970s. Monks and nuns participated in the work of helping refugees, orphans, and the wounded. In the situation of war, a monk cannot just sit in the meditation hall while bombs are being dropped all around. The bombs may fall on his temple as well. The heart of Buddhist meditation is mindfulness—

the energy that helps us know what is happening in the present moment. If what is happening in the present moment is the destruction of human lives, the monk should engage himself in the work of helping and caring. This is a concrete expression of compassion.

The question is not whether to be engaged or not. The question is how to engage without losing the contemplative life. The teaching of the *Satipatthana Sutta* says that this is possible. How can we carry on the labor of love without losing the practice? Listen to Mother Teresa: "Our Sisters must walk the street, take the streetcar as other people do, and enter the houses of the poor. We cannot enclose ourselves behind walls and wait for the poor to knock at our door. . . . We are street people. Our Sisters walk the streets and they pray as they walk. Sometimes they tell me how much time it took to reach a place, they tell me how many rosaries they said—three rosaries, four rosaries. They walk so rapidly that in Calcutta they are called 'the racing Sisters.' " Imagine how difficult it is to walk fast and to say rosaries at the same time! The pressure is always there. In the Buddhist tradition, there is the practice of walking meditation. We walk because we have to go somewhere, but we walk in a way that brings us calm, stability, and joy with each step. The question is how to structure our lives so that we do each thing in mindfulness, without losing our practice.

∽

MINDFUL LIVING IS POSSIBLE

Contemplation and action go well together if the monk knows how to organize his daily life. One day of mindfulness every week is essential. This goes well with the spirit of the Sabbath. The best way to practice is with a Sangha: the collective energy of mindfulness deepens the practice. The presence of the Sangha is a protection and an empowerment, and this presence sustains us during the rest of the week as well. The monk practices mindful breathing while performing his daily tasks, eats silently in mindfulness, washes his bowl as though he is bathing the baby Buddha, practices taking refuge in the Three Jewels in every moment, helps the sick and the wounded as though he is serving a Buddha or a bodhisattva, and looks deeply at each object he comes into contact with—an orange, a raindrop, a leaf, or a dying person. After several years of training, this is possible, especially if the monk lives and works in a Sangha where others are following the same practice. I know a monk who was mindful of his breathing and of every step he made throughout an entire teaching tour of one hundred days in one of the busiest societies in the world.

∽

OUR ORIGINAL PURPOSE

In *Crossing the Threshold of Hope,* Pope John Paul II wrote, "The Pope prays as the Holy Spirit permits him to pray." For me, the Holy Spirit is mindfulness itself. How can someone pray without mindfulness? He also wrote, "Man will not cross the threshold of truth without the help of the Holy Spirit. Prayer for the suffering and with the suffering is therefore a special part of this great cry that the Church and the Pope raise together with Christ." I believe that if anyone, Buddhist or Christian, embraces suffering with his or her own mindfulness or allows the Holy Spirit to work within himself, he will come to really understand the nature of that suffering and will no longer impose on himself or others dogmas that constitute obstacles for working toward the cessation of that suffering.

When we are caught in notions, rituals, and the outer forms of the practice, not only can we not receive and embody the spirit of our tradition, we become an obstacle for the true values of the tradition to be transmitted. We lose sight of the true needs and actual suffering of people, and the teaching and practice, which were intended to relieve suffering, now cause suffering. Narrow, fundamentalist, and dogmatic practices always alienate people, especially those who are suffering. We have to remind ourselves again and again of our original purpose, and the original teachings and intention of Buddha, Jesus, and other great sages and saints.

❧

THE WELL IS WITHIN US

In Buddhism, the source of our energy is faith in our daily practice. Faith in an *idea* is too risky. Ideas can change, even ideas about the Buddha. Tomorrow we may not believe the same thing, and we may fall into the abyss of doubt. We know very well that our daily practice of mindful living has brought us joy and peace, and so we have faith and confidence in our practice. It is a kind of experiential faith. We know that when we practice walking mindfully, we refresh ourselves, and we feel peace and joy with every step. No one can remove this from us because we have tasted the reality. This kind of faith gives us real strength.

In Buddhism, we speak of touching nirvana with our own body. In Christianity, you can also touch the Kingdom of God with your body, right here and now. It is much safer than placing our hope in the future. If we cling to our idea of hope in the future, we might not notice the peace and joy that are available in the present moment. The best way to take care of the future is to take care of the present moment. Practicing conscious breathing, aware of each thought and each act, we are reborn, fully alive, in the present moment. We needn't abandon our hope entirely, but unless we channel our energies toward being aware of what is going on in the present moment, we might not discover the peace and happiness that are available right now. The well is within us. If we dig deeply in the present moment, the water will spring forth.

RELIGIOUS EXPERIENCE IS HUMAN EXPERIENCE

I have noticed that Christians and Buddhists who have lived deeply their contemplative lives always come to express themselves in more non-dualistic, non-dogmatic ways. Christian mystics and Zen masters never sound speculative or intellectual. A dialogue between a Christian mystic and a Zen master would not be difficult to understand. Their speculative minds have given way to a nondiscursive spirit. Because they have learned not to get caught in notions or representations, they do not speak as though they alone hold the truth, and they do not think that those in other traditions are going the wrong way.

Religious experience is inevitably human experience. It has to do with the human consciousness, both individual and collective. In Buddhism, religious practice begins with mindfulness. As the practice deepens and mindfulness becomes more sustained, the practitioner is able to touch, feel, see, and understand more deeply. Understanding makes love and compassion possible, and when love and compassion are present, understanding deepens. The practitioner learns how to practice to maintain mindfulness and help it grow. She knows that while mindfulness is alive, transformation can take place.

Those who know how to dwell in mindfulness, the sutra says, are the ones who live in the house of the Tathagata, wear the Tathagata's clothes, and eat the Tathagata's food. They dwell in peace and security. But our habit energies are strong, and we have the tendency to be overcome by dispersion and forgetfulness, the opposites of mindfulness. The moment we become lost in forgetfulness, we stop dwelling in the house of the Tathagata. King Tran Thai Tong of thirteenth-century Vietnam wrote, "You are invited to stay in the house of the Tathagata, but your habit energy makes you sleep night after night among the reeds." The Buddhist way of handling habit energy is to be aware of it each time it arises. The moment we are aware of it, it already begins to transform. But training in mindfulness practice is needed for us to succeed.

∞

LOVING GOD IS LOVING LIVING BEINGS

I like the expression "resting in God." When you pray with all your heart, the Holy Spirit is in you, and as you continue to pray, the Holy Spirit continues in you. You do not need to do anything else. As long as the Holy Spirit is there, everything is fine. You are resting in God, and God will work in you. For transformation to take place, you only need to allow the Holy Spirit to stay in you. The Holy Spirit is the energy of God that shines forth and shows you the way. You can see things deeply, understand deeply, and love deeply.

If practiced in this way, the Lord's Prayer can bring about real transformation: "Our Father who art in Heaven, Hallowed be Thy name, Thy Kingdom come, Thy will be done, on Earth as it is in Heaven." A Buddhist would understand this as touching the ultimate dimension and realizing that the ultimate dimension and the historical dimension are one. It is like the wave touching the water, which is its own nature. This touching removes fear, anger, anxiety, and craving. Heaven and earth become one. "Give us this day our daily bread and forgive us our trespasses, as we forgive those who trespass against us. Lead us not into temptation, but deliver us from evil." The Lord's Prayer shows us that loving God is loving the living beings we see and touch in our daily life. If we can love them, we can love God.

∞

EMPTY OF WHAT?

Mindfulness, the capacity to be here, to witness deeply everything that happens in the present moment, is the beginning of enlightenment. The same is true of the Holy Spirit. Buddhists say that everyone has the seed of mindfulness in the deepest level of his or her consciousness, and that the practice helps that seed to manifest. This seed of mindfulness is the presence of the Buddha in us, called Buddha nature *(Buddhata)*, the nature of enlightenment. Christians say that God is in everyone's heart. The Holy Spirit can be described as being always present in our hearts in the form of a seed. Every time we pray or invoke the name of the Lord, that seed manifests itself as the energy of God. The Kingdom of God is in us as a seed, a mustard seed. If we cannot accept this, why do we say that God is within us?

As the lamp is lit, we begin to see things within us and around us more deeply. According to the teachings of Buddhism, it is important to look deeply into things and discover their nature of impermanence *(anitya)* and non-self *(anatman)*. Impermanence and non-self are not negative. They are the doors that open to the true nature of reality. They are not the causes of our pain. It is our delusion that causes us to suffer. Regarding something that is impermanent as permanent, holding to something that is without self as having a self, we suffer. Impermanence is the same as non-self. Since phenomena are impermanent, they do not possess a permanent identity. Non-self is also emptiness. Emptiness of what? Empty of a permanent self. Non-self means also interbeing. Because everything is made of everything else, nothing can be by itself alone. Non-self is also interpenetration, because everything contains everything else. Non-self is also interdependence, because this is made of that. Each thing depends on all other things to be. That is interdependence. Nothing can be by itself alone. It has to inter-be with all other things. This is non-self.

∾

THE NATURE OF INTERBEING

Mindfulness and concentration lead to a direct experience of impermanence and non-self, so that impermanence and non-self are no longer notions and images, but a direct experience. A Zen monk said, "Before I began to practice, mountains were mountains, and rivers were rivers. During many years of practice, mountains stopped being mountains and rivers stopped being rivers. Now as I understand things properly, mountains are mountains, and rivers are rivers." Thanks to the practice, this monk was able to see the nature of interbeing. He was no longer caught by the notions of self and non-self. Some people say that Buddhist practice is to dissolve the self. *They do not understand that there is no self to be dissolved. There is only the notion of self to be transcended.*

As soon as you know mountains are made of rivers and everything else and rivers are made of mountains and everything else, it is safe for you to use the words "mountains" and "rivers." In Buddhist practice, what is essential is for you to realize the nature of interbeing and transcend the notion of self and all its constraints. When you touch the reality of non-self, you touch at the same time nirvana, the ultimate dimension of being, and become free from fear, attachment, illusion, and craving.

THE GROUND OF
EXPERIENCE

It is necessary to die in order to be reborn. As soon as you experience impermanence, non-self, and interbeing, you are born again. But if the plant does not become dormant in the winter, it cannot be reborn in the spring. Jesus said that unless you are reborn as a child, you cannot enter the Kingdom of God. Thomas Merton wrote, "The living experience of divine love and the Holy Spirit . . . is a true awareness that one has died and risen in Christ. It is an experience of mystical renewal, an inner transformation brought about entirely by the power of God's merciful love, implying the 'death' of the self-centered and self-sufficient ego and the appearance of a new and liberated self who lives and acts in the Spirit." It would be impossible for a monk or a layperson to have this experience if she does not practice resting in God, if she only takes refuge in work, losing herself in it. Whether the practice is *psalmodia, lectio, oratio, contemplatio,* or *meditatio,* the true presence of the Holy Spirit in one's being is the ground that makes this experience possible, even if we affirm that the experience is a gift of God.

∾

CONCRETE PRAYER

The beginner's mind, the mind of love or the mind of enlightenment *(bodhicitta),* is absolutely essential for the Buddhist practitioner. It is the source of energy that helps the monk focus all his being on the practice. The career of the practitioner is the career of enlightenment. Enlightenment here means touching the ultimate, nirvana. Daily practice helps consolidate that mind and prevent it from being eroded. If his mind of enlightenment is strong, the monk will follow the path of practice naturally, like water flowing in a stream. In Buddhism, this is called "stream-winning." Anything the monk encounters after entering the stream becomes the object of his meditation: a floating cloud, a corpse, even his own fear. His deep concentration helps him touch and penetrate the objects of his meditation and reveal their true nature. Monks or laypersons who practice well always observe the Five Wonderful Precepts, the 58 Bodhisattva Precepts, or the 250 Pratimoksa Precepts. These guidelines are the expression of the practitioner's understanding and love. They are not rules imposed from the outside. They are the concrete practices of mindfulness that help him focus his entire being on the object of his meditation. Precepts *(sila)* make concentration *(samadhi)* possible, and concentration brings about enlightenment (prajña). Enlightenment is the breaking through to the true nature of reality.

Observing the Ten Commandments in daily life is also the concrete practice of prayer and meditation. Prayer of the Heart is not possible for one who does not consistently observe the commandments. If you do not observe, for example, "Thou shalt not kill," how can "Thou shall love the Lord thy God" be possible?

∾

TOTAL SURRENDER

The true nature of things is called, in Buddhism, cessation (nirodha) or extinction (nirvana). Cessation is first of all the cessation of all notions and illusions, and extinction is the extinction of notions and wrong perceptions. The extinction of delusion brings about the cessation of craving, anger, and fear, and the manifestation of peace, solidity, and freedom. All notions applied to the phenomenal world—such as creation, destruction, being, non-being, one, many, coming, and going—are transcended. The greatest relief we can obtain is available when we touch the ultimate, Tillich's "ground of being." We no longer identify our body's duration as our lifetime. We no longer think that life begins when we are born or stops when we die, because the notions of birth and death have been transcended. Life is no longer confined to time and space. This is the practice of releasing the notion "lifetime."

Touching nirvana, touching the ultimate dimension, is a total and unconditional surrender to God. If the wave knows that its ground of being is water, it overcomes all fear and sorrow. The moment the monk surrenders his entire being to God as the

ground of being, all of his fears vanish. Listen to
Thomas Merton: "In the language of the monastic
fathers, all prayers, reading, meditation, and all the
activities of the monastic life are aimed at purity of
heart, an unconditioned and totally humble surrender to God, a total acceptance of ourselves and of
our situation as willed by Him. It means the renun-
ciation of all deluded images of ourselves, all exag-
gerated estimates of our own capacities, in order to
obey God's will as it comes to us."

∽

TWO TYPES OF
CAUSATION

Once the ultimate is touched, all notions are
transcended: birth, death, being, non-being, before,
after, one, many, and so forth. Questions like "Does
God exist?" or "Does nirvana exist?" are no longer
valid. God and nirvana as concepts have been transcended. Existence (being) and non-existence (non-
being) as concepts have also been transcended. Even
one notion (God/nirvana) is enough to block access
to the ultimate, so why add another (existence/not-
existence)? For the one who has had an experience
of God or nirvana, the question "Does God exist?"
is an indication of the lack of insight. All soteriolo-

gies belong at first to the historical dimension. But as one's observation gets deeper and the ultimate dimension is touched, the notions of beginning and ending are transcended.

According to Buddhism, there are two types of causality: causation within the historical dimension and causation between the historical dimension and the ultimate dimension. When we say, "I was born from my parents, and I was raised and nourished by my family and society," we are speaking about causation within the historical dimension. When we say, "Waves are born from water," we are speaking about causation as relationship between the historical dimension and the ultimate dimension. When Jesus called Himself the Son of Man, He was speaking of causation in terms of the historical dimension. When He referred to Himself as the Son of God, He was speaking of the relationship between the historical and the ultimate. We cannot speak of the ultimate in terms of the historical. We cannot treat the noumena, the ontological ground, as a detail or aspect of the phenomena. The Father-Son relationship is not the father-son relationship. God does not make the world in the way a baker makes bread. *Samsara* and nirvana are two dimensions of the same reality. There is a relationship, but it is a phenomena-noumena relationship, not a phenomena-phenomena one. Buddhists are aware of that. That is why they speak of "the separate investigation of noumena *(svabhava)* and phenomena *(laksana)*." And yet, at the same time, they are aware that the two realms are one.

Let us listen to the *Quicumque vult* from the Book of Common Prayer:

"And the Catholic Faith is this: that we worship one God in Trinity, and Trinity in Unity.

Neither confounding the Persons nor dividing the Substance.

For there is one Person of the Father, another of the Son, and another of the Holy Ghost.

But the Godhead of the Father, of the Son, and of the Holy Ghost is all one: the Glory equal, the majesty co-eternal.

Such as the Father is, such is the Son; and such is the Holy Ghost.

The Father uncreate, the Son uncreate, and the Holy Ghost uncreate.

The Father eternal, the Son eternal, and the Holy Ghost eternal . . .

So the Father is God the Son is God; and the Holy Ghost is God.

And yet they are not three Gods; but one God . . .

> The Father is made of none: neither created, nor begotten.
>
> The Son is of the Father alone: not made, nor created but begotten.
>
> The Holy Ghost is of the Father and of the Son, neither made nor created, nor begotten, but proceeding.
>
> For the right Faith is that we believe and confess: that our Lord Jesus Christ, the Son of God, is God and Man: God, of the substance of the Father, begotten before the worlds; and Man, of the substance of his mother, born in the world;
>
> Perfect God, and perfect Man: of a reasonable soul and human flesh subsisting;
>
> Equal to the Father, as touching his Godhead; and inferior to the Father, as touching his manhood.''

The insight of interbeing, the nature of non-self, can be touched when you hear this prayer. The same insight can also be obtained when you contemplate phenomena—a magnolia, a squirrel, or a cloud.

∞

WHO IS NOT UNIQUE?

John Paul II, in *Crossing the Threshold of Hope*, insists that Jesus is the only Son of God: "Christ is absolutely original and absolutely unique. If He were only a wise man like Socrates, if He were a 'prophet' like Muhammed, if He were 'enlightened' like Buddha, without any doubt He would not be what He is. He is the one mediator between God and humanity." This statement does not seem to reflect the deep mystery of the oneness of the Trinity. It also does not reflect the fact that Christ is also the Son of Man. All Christians, while praying to God, address Him as Father. Of course Christ is unique. But who is not unique? Socrates, Muhammed, the Buddha, you, and I are all unique. The idea behind the statement, however, is the notion that Christianity provides the only way of salvation and all other religious traditions are of no use. This attitude excludes dialogue and fosters religious intolerance and discrimination. It does not help.

∽

THE DIFFERENCE IS
IN EMPHASIS

It is a natural tendency of man to personify qualities like love, freedom, understanding, and also the ultimate. In Buddhism, the Perfection of Wisdom (Prajñaparamita) is described as the Mother of all Buddhas, and Indian Buddhists did represent it in

the form of a female person. The teaching of the
Buddha, the Dharma, is also represented as a body,
the Dharmakaya. Buddhists make offerings to the
historical Buddha as well as to the Dharmakaya. But
they know that Dharmakaya is not a person in the
sense of the five aggregates: form, feelings, perceptions, mental states, and consciousness. It is like
Freedom being personified as a Goddess. Freedom is
not a body made of the five aggregates. The ultimate
can be represented as a person, but the ultimate cannot be just an assembly of the five aggregates. The
true body of Jesus is His teaching. The only way to
touch Him is to practice His teaching. The teaching
of Jesus is His living body, and this living body of
Christ manifests itself whenever and wherever His
teaching is practiced.

Buddhists and Christians alike, in dialogue, want
to recognize similarities as well as differences in their
traditions. It is good that an orange is an orange and
a mango is a mango. The colors, the smells, and the
tastes are different, but looking deeply, we see that
they are both authentic fruits. Looking more deeply,
we can see the sunshine, the rain, the minerals, and
the earth in both of them. Only their manifestations
are different. Authentic experience makes a religion
a true tradition. Religious experience is, above all,

human experience. If religions are authentic, they contain the same elements of stability, joy, peace, understanding, and love. The similarities as well as the differences are there. They differ only in terms of emphasis. Glucose and acid are in all fruits, but their degrees differ. We cannot say that one is a real fruit and the other is not.

∞

REAL DIALOGUE BRINGS TOLERANCE

The absence of true experience brings forth intolerance and a lack of understanding. Organized religions, therefore, must create conditions that are favorable for true practice and true experience to flower. Authentic ecumenical practices help different schools within a tradition learn from one another and restore the best aspects of the tradition that may have been eroded. This is true within both Buddhism and Christianity. Today in the West, all schools of Buddhism are present, and through their interactions with one another, mutual learning is taking place, and the elements that have been lost in one tradition can be revived by another. The Roman Catholic church, the Eastern Orthodox church, and the Protestant churches could do the same. And it is possible to go even further. Different religious traditions can engage in dialogue with one another in a true spirit of ecumenism. Dialogue can be fruitful and enriching if both sides are truly open. If they really believe that there are valuable elements in each other's tradition and that they can learn from one another, they will also rediscover many valuable aspects of their own tradition through such an encounter. Peace will be a beautiful flower blooming on this field of practice.

Real dialogue makes us more open-minded, tolerant, and understanding. Buddhists and Christians both like to share their wisdom and experience. Sharing in this way is important and should be encouraged. But sharing does not mean wanting others to abandon their own spiritual roots and embrace your faith. That would be cruel. People are stable and happy only when they are firmly rooted in their own tradition and culture. To uproot them would make them suffer. There are already enough people uprooted from their tradition today, and they suffer greatly, wandering around like hungry ghosts, looking for something to fill their spiritual needs. We must help them return to their tradition. Each tradition must establish dialogue with its own people first, especially with those young people who are lost and alienated. During the last fifteen years while sharing the Buddha's Dharma in the West, I always urged my Western friends to go back to their own traditions and rediscover the values that are there, those values they have not been able to touch before. The practice of Buddhist meditation can help them do so, and many have succeeded. Buddhism is made of non-Buddhist elements. Buddhism has no separate self. When you are a truly happy Christian, you are also a Buddhist. And vice versa.

We Vietnamese have learned these lessons from our own suffering. When Christian missionaries came to Vietnam several hundred years ago, they urged us to abandon the cult of ancestral worship and to abandon our Buddhist tradition. Later, when they offered to help us in refugee camps in Thailand and Hong Kong, they also urged us to give up our roots. The good will to help and to save us was there, but the correct understanding was not. People cannot be happy if they are rootless. We can enrich one another's spiritual lives, but there is no need to alienate people from their ancestors and their values. This situation calls for more understanding. Church authorities must strive to understand the suffering of their own people. The lack of understanding brings about the lack of tolerance and true love, which results in the alienation of people from the church. True understanding comes from true practice. Understanding and love are values that transcend all dogma.

GLOSSARY

anapanasati (Pali)—lit. "mindfulness of breathing in and breathing out"

anatman (Skt.)—non-self or not-self; means there is no independent existence separable from everything else

Anguttara Nikaya—one of the five collections of the Buddha's discourses preserved in the Pali language

anitya (Skt.)—impermanence; according to the Buddha, everything is impermanent.

apophatic theology—from the Greek *apophasis,* "denying," also known as "negative theology." Knowledge of God obtained by way of negating all that we say He is.

apostles—a. the twelve witnesses whom Jesus Christ sent forth to preach His Gospel to the world b. a missionary of the early Christian Church c. a leader of the first Christian mission to a country or region

apostolic—1. of, relating to, or contemporary with the twelve apostles 2. of or relating to the faith, teaching, or practice of the twelve apostles 3a. of or relating to a succesion of spiritual authority from the twelve apostles, regarded by Anglicans, Roman Catholics, Eastern Orthodox, and some others to have been perpetuated by successive ordinations of bishops and to be requisite for valid orders and administration of sacraments b. Roman Catholic church; of or relating to the pope as the successor of Saint Peter; papal

Arhat (Skt.)—a Buddhist adept who has overcome all afflictions; lit. "one who is worthy of our respect and support"

atman (Skt.)—self; basic teaching of Indian Brahman priests to which the Buddha reacted

Avalokitesvara—bodhisattva of compassion; bodhisattva of deep listening

avidya (Skt.)—ignorance, lit. "the lack of light"

baptism—1. a religious sacrament marked by the symbolic use of water and resulting in admission of the recipient into the community of Christians 2. a ceremony, a trial, or an experience by which one is initiated, purified, or given a name

bodhicitta (Skt.)—lit. "mind of enlightenment"; mind of love; deepest, innermost request to realize oneself and work for the well-being of all

bodhisattva (Skt.)—lit. "enlightenment-being"; one on the path to awakening who vows to forego complete enlightenment until he or she helps all other beings attain enlightenment

Buddha (Skt.)—fully enlightened one, from Skt. root *buddh*, "to wake up"

Buddha nature (Skt.: Buddhata)—the seed of mindfulness and enlightenment in every person, representing our potential to become fully awake

Buddhanusmrti (Skt.)—recollection of the Buddha; reflecting on the ten qualities of the Buddha; visualizing his marks of beauty, calm, and happiness; or evoking his name

Buddhology—study of the life of the Buddha

Christ—1. the Messiah or "Lord's Anointed," whose advent was the subject of Jewish prophecy and expectation 2. the title given to Jesus of Nazareth, as embodying the fulfillment of messianic prophecy and expectation; since earliest Christian times treated as a proper name

Christmas—the festival of the nativity of Christ, celebrated on December 25

Christology—1. the theological study of the person and deeds of Jesus 2. a doctrine or theory based on Jesus or Jesus' teachings

concept—1. notion, idea, verbal, or theoretical description of reality formed in the mind, but not the reality itself. A general idea derived or inferred from specific instances or occurrences 2. the product of the faculty of conception; an idea or a class of objects, a general notion or idea

crucifixion—1. the act of crucifying, or of putting to death on a cross 2. the crucifying of Jesus Christ on Calvary 3. a representation of Jesus on the cross

dana (Skt.)—generosity, giving

Dharma (Skt.)—the way of understanding and love taught by the Buddha; lit. "the law"

Dharma doors—84,000 entries into the stream of the Buddha's teaching and realization

Dharmakaya (Skt.)—lit. "body of the Dharma," the body of the Buddha's teachings. Later it came to mean the glorious, eternal Buddha, who is always expounding the Dharma

engaged Buddhism—term coined in Vietnam emphasizing action based on awareness

enlightenment (Skt.: bodhi)—awakening. Enlightenment is always enlightenment about something

Eucharist—1. a sacrament and the central act of worship in many Christian churches, which was instituted at the Last Supper and in which bread and wine are consecrated and consumed in remembrance of Jesus' death; communion 2. the consecrated elements of this rite; from Greek *eukharistos,* grateful, thankful

evangelical—1. of, relating to, or in accordance with the Christian Gospel, especially one of the four Gospel books of the New Testament 2. of, relating to, or being a Protestant church that founds its teaching on the Gospel 3. of, relating to, or being a Christian church believing in the sole authority and inerrancy of the Bible, in salvation only through regeneration, and in a spiritually transformed personal life 4. characterized by ardent or crusading enthusiasm; zealous: an evangelical liberal; a member of an evangelical church or party; synonym: of missionaries or their work, apostolic, missionary

Gospel—1. the proclamation of the redemption preached by Jesus and the Apostles, which is the central content of Christian revelation 2. one of the first four books of the New Testament, describing the life, death, and resurrection of Jesus and recording his teaching 3. a teaching or doctrine of a religious teacher

Heaven—1. the abode of God, the angels, and the souls of those who are granted salvation 2. an eternal state of communion with God; everlasting bliss

Holy Spirit—1. the Third Person of the Christian Trinity 2. the energy sent by God

interbeing—the Buddhist teaching that nothing can be by itself alone, that everything in the cosmos must "inter-be" with everything else

Jesus—the given name of the teacher and prophet who lived in the first century of this era and whose life and teachings form the basis of Christianity. Christians believe Jesus to be the Son of God and the Christ; Hebrew: *Joshua*

karuna (Skt.)—compassion, helping to relieve suffering

laksana (Skt.)—marks, appearances, phenomenal aspects of reality

Last Supper—Passover Seder meal shared by Jesus and His disciples before His crucifixion

Mahayana—lit. "great vehicle"; northern schools of Buddhism that emphasize the compassionate action of bodhisattvas

Maitreya—the future Buddha, the Buddha of love

maitri (Skt.)—love, bringing joy

manifestation (Skt.: vijñapti)—when conditions are sufficient for the constituents of something to come together in a particular form that we can perceive

Manjusri—bodhisattva of understanding

mindfulness (Skt.: smrti)—the energy to be here and to witness deeply everything that happens in the present moment, aware of what is going on within and without

negative theology. See *apophatic theology*

Nirmanakaya—the transformation body of Shakyamuni Buddha

nirvana—extinction of ideas and concepts and of suffering based on ideas and concepts; the ultimate dimension of reality

nonduality—the nondiscriminative nature of all phenomena

noumenon (plural: noumena)—1. an object that can be intuited only by direct knowledge (intuition) and not perceived by the senses 2. an object independent of intellectual intuition of it or of sensuous perception of it. Also called thing-in-itself 3. in the philosophy of Kant, an object, such as the soul, that cannot be known through perception, although its existence can be demonstrated

ontology—1. the science or study of being; that department of metaphysics that relates to the being or essence of things, or to being in the abstract 2. discourse about the ground of being

Order of Interbeing—a socially engaged Buddhist order founded in Vietnam in 1965

Orthodox—1. adhering to the accepted or traditional and established faith, especially in religion 2. adhering to the Christian faith as expressed in the early Christian ecumenical creeds 3. of or relating to any of the churches or rites of the Eastern Orthodox church

phenomenon (plural: phenomena)—1. an occurrence, circumstance, or fact that is perceptible by the senses 2a. that which appears real to the mind, regardless of whether its underlying existence is proved or its nature understood b. in Kantian philosophy, the appearance of an object to the mind as opposed to its existence in and of itself, independent of the mind 3. in physics, an observable event

piety—1. the state or quality of being pious, especially: a. religious devotion and reverence to God b. devotion and reverence to parents and family: filial piety 2. a devout act, thought, or statement 3. an important word in Judaism emphasizing that all life is a reflection of God. From Latin for "dutiful conduct"

practice (Skt.: citta bhavana)—cultivating the mind and heart

prajña (Skt.)—understanding, wisdom

Prajñaparamita (Skt.)—lit. "understanding gone beyond"; Mahayana Buddhist literature developed in early years of Christian era, called Mother of All Buddhas

precepts (Skt.: sila)—1. rules or principles prescribing a particular course of action or conduct 2. guidelines offered by the Buddha to protect us and help us live in mindfulness

Pure Land—an ideal place to practice understanding and loving-kindness under the guidance of a Buddha

reincarnation—1. rebirth of the soul in another body 2. a rebirth in another form; a new embodiment

samadhi (Skt.)—concentration; an important component and also result of meditation practice

samatha (Skt.)—stopping, calming, tranquility; the first aspect of Buddhist meditation

Sambhogakaya—one of the three bodies of the Buddha according to Mahayana Buddhism; the body of bliss, or enjoyment

samsara (Skt.)—cycle of birth and death

Sangha (Skt.)—Buddhist community of practice comprised of monks, nuns, and laypersons. See *Three Jewels*

Sanskrit—Indian language in which most Mahayana Buddhist sutras were recorded

Seder (Heb.)—lit. "order, arrangement"; ritual meal commemorating the exodus of the Jews from Egypt, journey from bondage to freedom; celebrated the first two nights of Passover

Shakyamuni (Skt.)—name given to the Buddha after his enlightenment; lit. "sage of the Shakya clan"

Siddhartha Gautama (Skt.)—birth name of the Buddha, who lived in the 6th and 5th centuries B.C.

skandhas (Skt.)—five elements that comprise a human being according to the Buddha: form, feelings, perceptions, mental states, and consciousness

suchness (Skt.: tathata)—the true nature of things, or ultimate reality *sunyata (Skt.)*—emptiness, empty of a separate self. See *anatman* and *interbeing*

sutra—a scriptural narrative, especially a text traditionally regarded as a discourse of the Buddha or one of his disciples; lit. "thread"

Tathagata (Skt.)—lit. "one who comes from suchness" or "one who will return to suchness"; an epithet of the Buddha

tathagatagarbha (Skt.)—lit. "womb of the Tathagata"; the seed of mindfulness, enlightenment, and compassion that is in each of us

Thây—Vietnamese word for "teacher," used to address Buddhist monks in Vietnam

theologian—one who is learned in theology

theology—lit. "discourse about God" 1. the study of the nature of God and religious truth; rational inquiry into religious questions 2. a system or school of opinions concerning God and religious questions 3. a course of specialized religious study usually at a college or seminary

Theravada—lit. "way of the elders"; one of eighteen schools of early Buddhism, strongest today in south and southeast Asia

Three Jewels—Buddha, Dharma, Sangha; also known as Three Gems, Three Refuges

Trinity—the union of three divine persons, the Father, Son, and Holy Spirit, in one God

Vairochana—name of the Dharmakaya Buddha

Vedic—of or relating to the Vedas, the sacred writings of the Aryans, deemed canonical by later Hinduism *vipasyana (Skt.)*—insight, looking deeply; the second aspect of Buddhist meditation

walking meditation—walking mindfully, aware of each step and each breath, the way the Buddha walked

Zen—school of Mahayana Buddhism that emphasizes meditation as its primary practice

For information about Thich Nhat Hanh's retreat community in France, please contact:

Plum Village
Meyrac
47120 Loubès-Bernac, France

For a complete list of books and tapes by Thich Nhat Hanh and a schedule of his retreats and lectures worldwide, contact:

Parallax Press
P.O. Box 7355
Berkeley, California 94707